The Tyndale New Testament Commentaries

General Editor:
THE REV. CANON LEON MORRIS, M.Sc., M.Th., Ph.D.

PHILIPPIANS

D1102007

For
MARK CHARLES
and
KRISTIN JOY
with the hope
that in due time
they too will 'stand
firm in the Lord'
(Phil. 4:1)

THE EPISTLE OF PAUL
TO THE
PHILIPPIANS

AN INTRODUCTION AND COMMENTARY

by

RALPH P. MARTIN, M.A., Ph.D.

Professor of New Testament and Director of Graduate Studies Program,
Fuller Theological Seminary, Pasadena, California

Inter-Varsity Press
Leicester, England

William B. Eerdmans Publishing Company
Grand Rapids, Michigan

Inter-Varsity Press
38 De Montfort Street, Leicester LE1 7GP, England

Wm. B. Eerdmans Publishing Company
255 Jefferson S.E., Grand Rapids, MI 49503

Published and sold only in the USA and Canada by Wm. B. Eerdmans Publishing Co.

First edition 1959
Second edition 1987

Unless otherwise stated, quotations from the Bible are taken from the HOLY BIBLE: NEW INTERNATIONAL VERSION. Copyright © 1978 by the International Bible Society, New York. Published in Great Britain by Hodder and Stoughton Ltd, and used by permission of Zondervan Bible Publishers, Grand Rapids, Michigan.

British Library Cataloguing in Publication Data

Martin, Ralph P.
  The Epistle of Paul to the Philippians:
  an introduction and commentary.—
  2nd ed.—(The Tyndale New Testament commentaries; v.11)
  1. Bible. N.T. Philippians—Commentaries
  I. Title   II. Series
  227′.607   BS2705.3

IVP EDITION 0-85111-880-1

Library of Congress Cataloging in Publication Data

Reprinted, June 1989

EERDMANS EDITION 0-8028-0310-5

Set in Palatino
Typeset in Great Britain by Parker Typesetting Service, Leicester
Printed in USA by Eerdmans Printing Company, Grand Rapids, Michigan

Inter-Varsity Press is the publishing division of the Universities and Colleges Christian Fellowship (formerly the Inter-Varsity Fellowship), a student movement linking Christian Unions in universities and colleges throughout the United Kingdom and the Republic of Ireland, and a member movement of the International Fellowship of Evangelical Students. For information about local and national activities write to UCCF, 38 De Montfort Street, Leicester LE1 7GP.

GENERAL PREFACE

The original *Tyndale Commentaries* aimed at providing help for the general reader of the Bible. They concentrated on the meaning of the text without going into scholarly technicalities. They sought to avoid 'the extremes of being unduly technical or unhelpfully brief'. Most who have used the books agree that there has been a fair measure of success in reaching that aim.

Times, however, change. A series that has served so well for so long is perhaps not quite as relevant as when it was first launched. New knowledge has come to light. The discussion of critical questions has moved on. Bible-reading habits have changed. When the original series was commenced it could be presumed that most readers used the Authorized Version and one could make one's comments accordingly, but this situation no longer obtains.

The decision to revise and up-date the whole series was not reached lightly, but in the end it was thought that this is what is required in the present situation. There are new needs, and they will be better served by new books or by a thorough up-dating of the old books. The aims of the original series remain. The new commentaries are neither minuscule nor unduly long. They are exegetical rather than homiletic. They do not discuss all the critical questions, but none is written without an awareness of the problems that engage the attention of New Testament scholars. Where it is felt that formal consideration should be given to such questions, they are discussed in the Introduction and sometimes in Additional Notes.

But the main thrust of these commentaries is not critical. These books are written to help the non-technical reader to understand his Bible better. They do not presume a knowledge of Greek, and all Greek words discussed are transliterated; but the authors have the Greek text before them and their comments are made on the basis of the originals. The authors are free to choose their own modern translation, but are asked to bear in mind the variety of translations in current use.

The new series of *Tyndale Commentaries* goes forth, as the former series did, in the hope that God will graciously use these books to help the general reader to understand as fully and clearly as possible the meaning of the New Testament.

LEON MORRIS

CONTENTS

AUTHOR'S PREFACE TO THE FIRST EDITION

'Other men laboured, and ye are entered into their labours.' In no other sphere is the Lord's word to His disciples more applicable than in the task of biblical commentating. The present writer would acknowledge his great debt to his predecessors in the field, and place on record his appreciation of the works on which he has been glad to draw. Whereas in many places where opinions differ he has sought to make up his own mind as regards the varying interpretations which these earlier commentators offer, in some matters (in particular the vexed problem of the dating of the Epistle) he has been content to state the possibilities and to leave the reader to draw his own conclusions.

He would also like to express his gratitude to past teachers and present friends who have helped him in the preparation of this small work. The late Professor T. W. Manson was kind enough to give advice and encouragement in the initial stages of the work; and his lectures at Manchester and his assistance in post-graduate study have left an indelible mark. Mr R. F. Broadfoot, B.A., of Dunstable Grammar School, has read the MS, and has often helped in the elucidation of turgid German sentences in commentaries which have been consulted. Professor A. M. Hunter of Aberdeen has been helpful in answering queries, especially in the field of pre-Pauline Christianity, a study to which he has made his own distinctive contribution. Both he and the librarians of the Bedfordshire County Library and Dr Williams's Library in London have assisted with the loan of an occasional *recherché* volume, while a grant from the Particular Baptist Fund made possible the purchase of a number of important reference works which otherwise might not have been obtained.

The writing of the Commentary, together with the preparation of a special study on the Hymn of Philippians ii. 5–11,[1] has occupied most of the author's leisure time during the last two years. He can find no more fitting way of acknowledging the co-operation and help received from his church, where he has served as minister for six happy years, than to offer this work as a tribute to their loyalty and friendship. In the bond which has joined pastor and people at West Street Baptist Church, Dunstable, 'fellowship in the gospel', which, as we know from this Epistle, meant so much to the apostle Paul, has been a very real and memorable experience.

September, 1959 RALPH P. MARTIN

[1]Given as the 1959 Tyndale New Testament Lecture and published as a monograph by the Tyndale Press under the title *An Early Christian Confession: Philippians ii. 5–11 in Recent Interpretation* (London, 1960).

PREFACE TO THE SECOND EDITION

Over a quarter of a century has elapsed since this commentary appeared in its first edition. During that time several notable studies of Paul's Philippian letter have been written, and I have drawn gratefully on these resources which are listed and acknowledged in the revised bibliography.

In particular Paul's relations with the church at Philippi have been investigated with a view to showing the nature of the opposition to the gospel against which he warns in chapter 3. Also prominent in recent research has been the detailed study on the 'Christ hymn' in 2:6–11, with its portrayal of the way taken by the incarnate Lord to the cross and his enthronement as universal ruler of all life. Students of the apostle have helped us to see in clearer focus how the first believers hailed Jesus, at the dawn of apostolic history, as worthy of worship and the rightful Lord of the cosmos. These are matters of timely significance in the final decades of the twentieth century.

The revised commentary represents a rethinking of many other matters of exegetical and practical significance in the letter, and references to recent discussion have been added. At the same time, I have tried to keep the commentary as clear and readable as possible, so all who use it may be assisted and not mystified. The use of the New International Version has helped to this end, but whether I have in fact succeeded in these improvements must be left to the reader's judgment. The revised edition is sent out with the author's hope that it may indeed promote 'fellowship in the gospel' and enhance 'joy in Christ', twin ideas so dear to Paul as he wrote this letter in the first place.

Thanks are expressed to J. David Jackson, my doctoral student in the Graduate Studies Program, who read the typescript, expertly prepared by Janet M. Gathright, also a student in the doctoral program.

RALPH P. MARTIN

CHIEF ABBREVIATIONS

GENERAL

Abbott-Smith *A Manual Greek Lexicon of the New Testament* by G. Abbott-Smith, 1937.

AV/KJV English Authorized Version (King James).

BAGD *A Greek-English Lexicon of the New Testament* by W. Bauer. Translated and edited by W. F. Arndt, F. W. Gingrich and F. W. Danker, 2nd ed., 1979.

BJRL Bulletin of the John Rylands Library.

BZNTW Beihefte to *ZNTW*.

CBQ *Catholic Biblical Quarterly.*

ET English Translation.

EQ *The Evangelical Quarterly.*

ExpT *The Expository Times.*

GNB *Good News Bible (Today's English Version)*, 1976.

IBD *Illustrated Bible Dictionary*, eds. J. D. Douglas and N. Hillyer, 1980.

JB *The Jerusalem Bible*, 1966.

LXX Septuagint Version.

Moffatt *A New Translation of the Bible* by James Moffatt, 1935.

Moulton-Milligan *The Vocabulary of the Greek New Testament* by J. H. Moulton and G. Milligan, 1914–1930.

NCB *New Century Bible*, London and Grand Rapids.

NEB *The New English Bible*, 1970.

NIV *The New International Version*, 1978.

NovT *Novum Testamentum.*

NTS | *New Testament Studies.*
Phillips | *Letters to Young Churches* by J. B. Phillips, 1947.
RSV | Revised Standard Version, Old Testament, 1952; New Testament, ²1971.
RV | English Revised Version, 1881.
SNTSMS | Society for New Testament Studies Monograph Series, Cambridge.
TDNT | *Theological Dictionary of the New Testament*, eds. G. Kittel & G. Friedrich, trans. G. W. Bromiley, 1964–75.
ZNTW | *Zeitschrift für neutestamentliche Wissenschaft.*
1QS | *Rule of the Community* at Qumran.
1QM | *War Scroll* at Qumran.

COMMENTARIES IN ENGLISH

Beare | *A Commentary on the Epistle to the Philippians* by F. W. Beare, 1959.
Bruce | *Philippians* by F. F. Bruce (A Good News Commentary), 1983.
Caird | *Paul's Letters From Prison* by G. B. Caird (New Clarendon Bible), 1976.
Collange | *The Epistle of Saint Paul to the Philippians* by J. F. Collange, 1979.
Craddock | *Philippians* by Fred B. Craddock (Interpretation), 1985.
Getty | *Philippians and Philemon* by Mary Ann Getty (New Testament Message 14), 1980.
Grayston | *The Epistles to the Galatians and to the Philippians* by Kenneth Grayston (Epworth Preacher's Commentaries), 1957.
Hawthorne | *Philippians* by Gerald F. Hawthorne (Word Biblical Commentary), 1983.
Hendriksen | *A Commentary on the Epistle to the Philippians* by W. Hendriksen (Geneva Series), 1962.
Houlden | *Paul's Letters from Prison* by J. L. Houlden (Pelican New Testament Commentaries), 1970.
Kennedy | *The Epistle to the Philippians* by H. A. A. Kennedy

(Expositor's Greek Testament), 1903.

Lightfoot *Saint Paul's Epistle to the Philippians* by J. B. Lightfoot, 1896 ed.

Martin *Philippians* by Ralph P. Martin (New Century Bible) 1976, revised 1980.

Michael *The Epistle of Paul to the Philippians* by J. H. Michael (Moffatt New Testament Commentaries), 1928.

Motyer *The Message of Philippians* by J. A. Motyer (The Bible Speaks Today), 1984.

Moule *The Epistle to the Philippians* by H. C. G. Moule (Cambridge Greek Testament), 1906.

Müller *The Epistles of Paul to the Philippians and to Philemon* by J. J. Müller (New London/International Commentary on the New Testament), 1955.

Scott *The Epistle to the Philippians* by E. F. Scott (Interpreter's Bible), 1955.

Synge *Philippians and Colossians* by F. C. Synge (Torch Bible Commentaries), 1951.

Vincent *The Epistles to the Philippians and Philemon* by M. R. Vincent (International Critical Commentaries), 1897.

Wilson *Philippians. A Digest of Reformed Comment* by Geoffrey B. Wilson, 1983.

COMMENTARIES IN OTHER LANGUAGES

Barth *Erklärung des Philipperbriefes* by Karl Barth, 1928. ET *The Epistle to the Philippians*, 1962.

Bengel *Gnomon Novi Testamenti* by J. A. Bengel, 1742. ET *Gnomon of the New Testament*, 1862.

Benoit *Les Epîtres de Saint Paul aux Philippiens, etc.* by P. Benoit (La Bible de Jérusalem), 1949.

Bonnard *L'Epître de Saint Paul aux Philippiens* by P. Bonnard (Commentaire du Nouveau Testament), 1950.

Dibelius *An die Thessalonicher, i, ii; an die Philipper* by M. Dibelius (Handbuch zum Neuen Testament), 1937.

Gnilka	*Der Philipperbrief* (Herders Theologischer Kommentar zum NT) by J. Gnilka, 1968.
Heinzelmann	*Die kleineren Briefe des Apostels Paulus*, 8 (Das Neue Testament Deutsch); *Der Brief an die Philipper* by G. Heinzelmann, 1955.
Lohmeyer	*Der Brief an die Philipper* by E. Lohmeyer, ed. W. Schmauch (Meyer series), 1956.
Michaelis	*Der Brief des Paulus an die Philipper* by W. Michaelis (Theologischer Handkommentar zum Neuen Testament), 1935.

INTRODUCTION

I. THE CHURCH AT PHILIPPI

The establishment of the church at Philippi, marking, as it does, the entrance of the gospel of the Lord Jesus Christ into Europe, is described in Acts 16:12–40 with great fullness of detail. As a frontispiece to the narrative of Paul's coming and ministry Luke describes the city as 'a Roman colony and the leading city of that district of Macedonia' (Acts 16:12). This probably means that Philippi was the first city of the region or sub-province of Macedonia rather than the capital city, an honour which belonged to Thessalonica.[1] This statement is confirmed by what is known of Philippi from other sources.[2] Luke's full designation has been taken to mean that he had a special interest in the city, and even that it reflects his civic pride in his own place of origin.

The history of the site goes back at least to Philip II of Macedon about the year 360 BC. He gave the town its name (Philip's city) and fortified it. In 167 BC it became part of the Roman Empire, but its real importance was not achieved until after 31 BC. After Octavian defeated Antony and Cleopatra at the battle of Actium, Philippi 'received a settlement of Italian colonists who had favoured Antony and had been obliged to

---

[1] A. N. Sherwin-White, *Roman Society and Roman Law in the New Testament* (Oxford University Press, 1963), pp. 93 ff.

[2] For a full description of the archaeology of Philippi the works of P. Collart are authoritative: *Philippes, ville de Macédoine* (Paris, Ecole Française d'Athènes, Travaux et Mémoires, Fasc. v, 1937) and his article in *Dictionnarie d'Archéologie chrétienne et de Liturgie*, 14/1, 1939, pp. 712–741.

surrender their land to the veterans of Octavian'.[1] The full title of the city now appears as *Colonia Iulia Augusta Philippensis*. The dignity of Philippi as a Roman *colonia* is specially mentioned in Acts 16:12 and is important for the background of the epistle.

Of all the benefits of this title, which included the use of Roman law in local affairs and sometimes exemption from tribute and taxation, the possession of the *ius Italicum* was the most coveted. This is defined as the privilege 'by which the whole legal position of the colonists in respect to ownership, transfer of land, payment of taxes, local administration, and law, became the same as if they were on Italian soil; as, in fact, by a legal fiction, they were'.[2] Consequently Philippi had cause for civic pride and its favoured position is reflected by many allusions in the letter.

The narrative in Acts bears witness to the presence of a Jewish community before the coming of the Christian missionaries (Acts 16:13);[3] and to these Jewish women who met for prayer the apostle addressed his message and received the response of faith as the Lord opened the heart of a woman named Lydia, who is described in terms which can mean that she was almost a proselyte of Judaism. It is interesting to recall the appeal of the Jewish faith to women,[4] and also the high status of women in Macedonia.[5] The church at Philippi also contained a proportion of women as we know from the mention of feminine names in 4:2–3.[6]

The two conversion stories which are reported in the

---

[1]K. Lake and H. J. Cadbury (edd.), *The Beginnings of Christianity*, 4 (Macmillan, 1933), p. 187.

[2]Lake and Cadbury, *ibid.*, p.190.

[3]For the archaeological details here *cf.* Collart, *Philippes, ville de Macédoine*, pp. 321 ff., 458 ff.

[4]'In the case of Jewish propagandism, it was found that it was the female heart that was most impressionable', E. Schürer, *A History of the Jewish People in the time of Jesus Christ*, 2.2 (T. & T. Clark, 1893), p. 308

[5]*Cf.* W. Tarn and G. T. Griffith, *Hellenistic Civilization* (E. Arnold, ³1952), pp. 98, 99, 'If Macedonia produced perhaps the most competent group of men the world had yet seen, the women were in all respects the men's counterparts; they played a large part in affairs, received envoys and obtained concession for them from their husbands, built temples, founded cities, engaged mercenaries, commanded armies, held fortresses, and acted on occasion as regents or even co-rulers.'

[6]W. D. Thomas, 'The Place of Women at Philippi', *ExpT*, 83, 1971–72, pp. 117–120.

remaining verses of Acts 16 make it clear that the gospel was not restricted to Jews or Jewish adherents. 'To the Jew first and also to the Greek' (Rom. 1:16, RSV) was the motto of the apostle's evangelistic procedure; and two notable conversions from the world of paganism are graphically recorded, the slave-girl (16:16–18) and the Roman jailer (vv. 19–34).

Both these incidents provide interesting background and information about the citizens of a city in which the infant Christian community was formed. The practice of soothsayers under the control of an oracular spirit, the yearning for 'salvation' (vv. 17, 30) and the intolerance shown towards the monotheism and morality of the Jews (v. 20) are evidence of the prevailing tendencies in the religious climate of this Graeco-Roman city.[1] Added to this, we observe their intense loyalty to the Roman ethos both as an occasion of proud conviction (v. 21) and also as a confession of disturbing fear when they realized that they had actually beaten and bound men who were Romans (v. 38). Sherwin-White, *Roman Society*, should be consulted for the issue of Roman patriotism which lies in the background of Paul's mission preaching at Philippi and the subsequent letter.

In such an atmosphere ('in a crooked and depraved generation', Phil. 2:15), a church was founded in circumstances which left an indelible mark on Paul's mind. His letter harks back to the 'first day' when God's good work began in the converts' lives (1:3–6). The time of his first visit was 'in the early days of . . . the gospel' (4:15), and since then he had known a continuance of the church's fellowship across the years. He looks upon them as his 'joy and crown' (4:1) and boasts of them to other churches (2 Cor. 8:1ff.).[2]

As to the composition of the church at Philippi, in spite of the explicit reference to the Lydian woman who had attach-

---

[1] See J. N. Sevenster, *The Roots of Pagan Anti-Semitism in the Ancient World* (Brill, 1975).

[2] See Polycarp's *Epistle to the Philippians*, 11:3 which refers to the apostle's praise for the Philippians: 'For about you he boasts in all the churches.' *Cf.* The 'Marcionite' Prologue to the Epistle: 'The Philippians are Macedonians. They persevered in faith after they had accepted the word of truth and they did not receive false prophets. The apostle praises them writing to them from Rome in prison by Epaphroditus.'

ment to Judaism, it seems clear that the main influx into the fellowship was from the Gentile world. Although the church was based on Lydia's house (Acts 16:40) the names of the church members in the letter (2:25; 4:2–3) show that the later converts were former pagans. Luke himself appears to have remained in Philippi after the apostle and his companions moved on – the 'we' section of Acts is not resumed until 20:6 when 'we sailed from Philippi' – and no doubt the presence of a Christian leader such as Luke was a powerful aid to evangelization and consolidation in the days which followed.

II. DATE AND PLACE OF COMPOSITION

1. A ROMAN ORIGIN

The traditional dating of the epistle is associated with the apostle's captivity at Rome (Acts 28:16, 30) and it is customary still to speak of Philippians as one of the Prison Epistles. As this imprisonment lasted for 'two whole years' the question arises: To which part of the captivity does the epistle belong? The view of Lightfoot[1] is that the letter is, in fact, the earliest of the Prison Epistles. His grounds are first, the linguistic affinity of Philippians with Romans; and second, its marked difference, on the grounds of content and language, from Colossians and Ephesians which are placed nearer the close of the period of Roman captivity.

Among the writers who champion the Roman dating, this relative placing of Philippians is almost universally rejected, on the following main grounds:

1. The journeys and communications between Rome and Philippi demand a reasonable interval of time. 2. The legal issue of the trial is still in the balance at the time of writing, and this points to the end of the captivity when Paul was tried and

---

[1]J. B. Lightfoot, *St Paul's Epistle to the Philippians*, ch. 2.

acquitted, or executed,[1] or exiled.[2] 3. Little weight of importance can be attached to the variations in the apostle's vocabulary and style. The use of different words in the other Prison Epistles may be explained largely on the score of different subject-matter, and we must bear in mind that the character of Philippians is more informal and personal than that of the other letters. The literary affinity with Romans is impressive, as Lightfoot has demonstrated, but here again this close agreement betokens merely a common author whose mind is addressed to similar topics in both letters.[3]

The dating of the epistle at the close of the Roman captivity rests upon the following grounds:

1. The writer is a prisoner[4] (see 1:7, 13–14, 17) and his imprisonment is serious (1:20ff.; 1:30; 2:17) because the issue of life or death is uncertain. It may result in Paul's release, which is his fervent hope for the sake of the Philippians (1:19, 23–24), or it may be a fatal issue which will be the sentence of death (1:20–23; 2:17) and the martyr's crown (3:11).

2. From the information given in the book of the Acts we know of only three imprisonments. These are Acts 16:23–40, at the time of Paul's first visit to Philippi; Acts 21:33 – 23:30, the arrest at Jerusalem, followed by two years' detention at Caesarea (24:27); and Acts 27 – 28:16, the voyage to Rome as a prisoner, followed by a further imprisonment of two years'

---

[1]Or possibly the case against him went by default. *Cf.* H. J. Cadbury's Note xxvi: 'Roman Law and the Trial of Paul' in *The Beginnings of Christianity*, 5, pp. 297 ff., and J. J. Gunther, *Paul: Messenger and Exile* (Judson, 1972) ch. 6.

[2]On balance, the most likely in my view: see R. P. Martin, *New Testament Foundations*, 2 (Paternoster/Eerdmans, 1978), pp. 298–300 incorporating the evidence in the Pastoral Epistles.

[3]*Cf.* G. S. Duncan's warning, *ExpT*, 67, 1956, p. 163: 'Theories of doctrinal development, like arguments based on literary affinities, ought not to have more than a secondary place in determining questions of historical sequence, and may, if applied without due caution, yield dangerously misleading results'; also W. Michaelis, *Die Datierung des Philipperbriefes* (Mohn, 1933), p.17, for the view that the dating of the letter must be fixed independently of language and style.

[4]T. W. Manson, *Studies in the Gospels and Epistles* (Manchester University Press, 1962), pp. 149–167, finds indications in the letter that Paul was at liberty when he wrote it. He regards the trial as already past. The apostle is now a free man, and his 'chains' are his continuing experiences of hardship in every place. This reading of 1:7, 12 ff., 16f., 30 can hardly be correct. These verses indicate that Paul's imprisonment is still going on at the time of writing.

duration (28:30). The epistle to the Philippians cannot have been written during the first; the case for a Caesarean origin (it is said) is weak and unconvincing; therefore it must have been written during the Roman imprisonment.

3. This is confirmed by references to the scene of Paul's captivity in 1:13: 'it has become clear throughout the whole palace guard . . . that I am in chains for Christ'. The original word *praitōrion* is taken by the NIV, which follows Lightfoot's conclusion here, to be the 'praetorian guard' at Rome; but for a difficulty in regard to the vast number of such praetorian soldiers, see the Commentary at 1:13.

A closing greeting is conveyed to the readers from those 'who belong to Caesar's household' (4:22). This is taken by Lightfoot and others to be an allusion to the imperial slaves or freedmen in the service of the emperor at the capital city.

There are, however, certain reservations which have made scholars pause before regarding the above conclusion as certain and indisputable. These difficulties may be enumerated as follows:

1. The menacing situation reflected in such verses as 1:20–23, 30; 2:17 with their indication that death was an imminent possibility for Paul hardly tallies with the comparative freedom and relaxed atmosphere at the close of Acts. If Philippians was written at Rome it is necessary to postulate an unfavourable development in the apostle's relations with the authorities which led to a change for the worse in his conditions and prospects: his circumstances would have altered from those of the 'free custody' (*libera custodia*), as it was called, in Acts 28 (*cf.* Eusebius, *Ecclesiastical History*, 2:22, 1) to those of strict confinement and the impending danger of Philippians 1:20ff., 30; 2:17.

To this obvious difference between the two situations there may be added the difference between the charge levelled at the apostle according to Philippians and that on which he was remitted to Rome. In the first case, the gravamen was the preaching of the word (1:13, 16); but in Jerusalem he was arrested because of his supposed violation of the Temple (Acts 21:28; 24:6; 25:8) and he is sent to Rome on this charge (*cf.* Acts

28:17).[1] So it is conjectured[2] that, while the charge of Temple violation (Acts 24:12) could be rebutted, there would be more serious charges levied against him, *e.g.* that he was a social offender (Acts 24:5), and there was no way of his knowing how the verdict would go.

2. Much has been made, chiefly by Deissmann,[3] who first elaborated the point, of the great distance and frequent journeys and communications between Philippi and Rome which are required by the internal evidence of the letter itself. He gives a list of no less than five journeys to and from the place of Paul's confinement, together with an extra four trips envisaged in the future plans of Paul. These are given as follows:

a. The journey of Timothy to Paul's side at the place of his captivity. He is not mentioned in the journey to Rome (Acts 26–28) but was with the apostle when the letter was composed (1:1).

b. A message from the scene of captivity to Philippi to say that Paul is a prisoner and is in need (4:14).

c. After the collection of a love gift at Philippi it is brought by Epaphroditus who travels from Philippi to the place of the imprisonment (4:18).

d. Epaphroditus falls sick, and news of this somehow[4] reaches the church at Philippi (2:26).

e. Paul now receives a message that the Philippians have heard of their messenger's sickness, and he is able to report that this news has had a painful effect upon Epaphroditus himself (2:26).

The journeys which are planned according to inferences in the letter are:

---

[1] *Cf.* P. Benoit, *Les épîtres de Saint Paul aux Philippiens, etc.*, pp. 11, 12.

[2] Bruce, *Philippians*, p. xxiv.

[3] A. Deissmann, 'Zur ephesinischen Gefangenschaft des Apostels Paulus', in *Anatolian Studies presented to Sir W. M. Ramsay*, ed. W. H. Buckler and W. M. Calder (Manchester University Press, 1923), pp. 121–127.

[4] It has been proposed that Epaphroditus fell sick en route to Paul's prison, and not when he had arrived at where Paul was. So B. S. MacKay, *NTS*, 7, 1960–61, pp. 161–170 and C. O. Buchanan, *EQ*, 36, 1964, pp. 157–166. This suggestion is based on 2:30, but it is weak, as we shall see.

a. Epaphroditus' journey to bring the letter to Philippi (2:25, 28).

b. Timothy's journey in the near future from the place of Paul's confinement to Philippi (2:19).

c. Journey b. will mean that when Timothy fulfils his mission he will return to Paul so that he 'may be cheered' when he learns of their state (2:19).

d. Paul's journey in the near future (2:24).

Deissmann remarks that 'those enormous journeys' cannot be fitted into the period of Acts 28:30, that the use of the adverbs 'soon' (2:19, 24) and 'immediately' (2:23) gives the impression that the distance between the place of writing and the city of Philippi is not great, and that such rapid and repeated travel is more likely to be possible, in the time of the imprisonment, if the apostle is captive at a place nearer to Philippi than Rome. He names Ephesus as the most likely alternative.

In reply to this argument based on distance and travel time which is used by those who oppose the traditional dating of the epistle it may be said that a lot depends upon the approximate calculation of the time taken to make the journey from Philippi to Rome.[1] Lightfoot gives this as a month,[2] but a period of seven to eight weeks would be more accurate. Even on this longer reckoning it is a fact that there is evidence of the relative speed and dependability of travel in the world of Paul's day,[3] and Dodd and Harrison feel that there is no difficulty in fitting these travel times into the two years of Acts 28:30.[4]

3. We may take note of the impression which the letter has made on several scholars that, since the foundation of the Philippian church, the apostle had not been to visit it up to the time

---

[1]A distance of 730 land miles plus one or two days' sea voyage across the Adriatic.

[2]Lightfoot, p. 38, note 1. P. N. Harrison, *Polycarp's Two Letters* (Cambridge University Press, 1936), pp. 113–116, discusses this calculation and comments: 'In order to accomplish the whole journey in 33 days ('about a month'), they would have needed to cover those 730 land miles in 31 days at an average speed rate of 23½ miles a day, with no halts' (p. 113). He shows that, using the example of Ignatius' journey, a period of forty-nine days is more feasible (p.116).

[3]See a study by L. Casson, *Travel in the Ancient World* (Hakkert, 1974), ch. 9, for the speed and reliability of travel in New Testament times.

[4]C. H. Dodd, *New Testament Studies* (Manchester University Press, 1953), pp. 96 ff.; P. N. Harrison, *NTS*, 2, 1956, p. 260.

when he wrote the epistle.[1] References in 1:30 and 4:15f. take the reader back to the days of the first missionary journey, and appear to indicate that Paul had not renewed acquaintance with the Philippian Christians since those days. But this cannot be so, if Paul is at Rome when he writes his letter, because he *has* visited the church since the first visit of Acts 16. Acts 20:1–6 records such return visits.

The reminiscence of 1:30 ('the same struggle you saw I had') suggests a shorter time than the eleven to twelve years which must have elapsed if Paul were writing from Rome; and a mention of the early days of their faith (1:5; 4:15) gives the impression that only a short time has intervened between Paul's first visit and preaching and the time of the letter.

4. Philippians 2:24 (*cf.* Phm. 22) expresses the hope and intention of the apostle to revisit the church if his release is granted. Now earlier verses (1:24–27) suggest that what he had in mind was not just an isolated visit, but rather the continuation of his missionary and pastoral work among the Philippians. This is an important indication of the apostle's outlook, because we know that at the time of Romans 15:23–24, 28 he considered his missionary work in the east as finished, and was setting his face in the direction of the west and thinking in terms of a projected visit to Spain. Now if, some years later than the writing of Romans 15:23–24, 28, Paul is found expressing the intention of revisiting Philippi we must suppose that a new situation has arisen which led him to change his missionary strategy.[2] While this is, of course, possible, it is also to be noted

[1] For example, W. Michaelis, *Der Brief des Paulus an die Philipper* (Deichert, 1935), p. 3. He finds this impression strengthened by 2:12 and 1:26. Other scholars (*e.g.* W. L. Knox, *St. Paul and the Church of the Gentiles* [Cambridge University Press, 1939], p. 180) form the exactly opposite impression from 4:15 f., and C. H. Dodd, *op. cit.*, p. 99 is unimpressed by this argument in favour of an earlier dating than the Roman one.

[2] For the view that Paul abandoned his plan to go to Spain, see A. Schlatter, *The Church in the New Testament Period* (ET, SPCK, 1955), pp. 220, 236. But this is improbable in the light of early Christian tradition, see G. Ogg, *The Chronology of the Life of Paul* (Epworth Press, 1968; U.S. title, *The Odyssey of Paul*, Revell), ch. 21. Dodd, *New Testament Studies*, p. 96 suggests that Paul changed his mind on the ground that, as he depended for his proposed Spanish mission on support from Rome, and as Philippians shows that a large section of the Roman church was opposed to him, he decided to postpone the projected enterprise of Romans 15 and revisit Philippi in view of the Jewish opposition there. Bruce, *Philippians*,

that if Philippians was brought back to a period before Acts 20 then we have a situation in which the promised visit of Philippians 1:26; 2:24 was fulfilled in Acts 19:21; 20:1ff., along with the pledge to send Timothy to the Philippians (2:19, 23) which was made good according to Acts 19:22; 1 Corinthians 4:17; 16:10f. On this view, the evidence of Romans 15 for a mission in the west also stands (*cf.* 1 Clement 5:5–7).

This correspondence between 'the persons concerned, the objective and the sequence of events of the journeys' is treated as a very impressive argument for pushing back the composition of the letter to a period into which it fits like the key piece of a jig-saw; and if the events do not correspond it is necessary to suppose a remarkable duplication.[1] On the other hand, there is no mention of Erastus in Philippians as there is in Acts 19:22 and Harrison finds a disparity in the reasons given for the missions of Timothy recorded in Acts 19:22 and Philippians 2:19.[2]

If the case for the Roman origin is open to criticism on the grounds which are outlined above, what better alternative is possible? Two or three suggested possibilities have been offered to overcome the difficulties which are felt, by some scholars, to stand in the way of the acceptance of the time-honoured order of the Pauline letters. One such option, that Paul wrote the letter from Corinth may be summarily mentioned – and dismissed.[3]

2. A CAESAREAN ORIGIN

This was first propounded by Oeder of Leipzig in 1713, and supported more recently by Pfleiderer, Spitta, Lohmeyer, J. A. T. Robinson[4] and G. F. Hawthorne and its claims re-opened for

---

p. xxiv grants that Paul's travel plans were never inflexible, noting that a change in plans from the date in Acts and Romans is inevitable on the hypothesis of a Roman origin of Philippians.

[1] W. Michaelis, *Einleitung in das Neue Testament* (Haller Verlag, ²1954), pp. 208, 209. See also G. S. Duncan, *St. Paul's Ephesian Ministry* (Hodder & Stoughton, 1929), pp. 77–80

[2] In *loc. cit.*, pp. 258–259; but see Duncan's answer in *NTS*, 3, 1957, p. 218.

[3] Details are given in Martin, *Philippians* (NCB, 1976=1980), pp. 44, 45.

[4] J. A. T. Robinson, *Redating the New Testament* (SCM, 1976), pp. 57–61. Evaluation of his arguments is in my *Philippians* (NCB, 1976=1980), pp. 45–48.

consideration. On this theory the imprisonment to which the letter refers would be located in Caesarea where Paul was detained according to Acts 23:33. Lohmeyer dates the epistle in the year AD 58 during the time of the apostle's detention at Caesarea, advancing the evidence of Acts 23:35 where Herod's 'palace' (lit. *praitōrion*: see RV margin) is named as the place of confinement.[1] This place he would equate with the *praitōrion* of Philippians 1:13. This identification *may* be so; but it may also be true of many other provincial cities throughout the Empire (*e.g.* Corinth). Certainly there is no necessity to trace this reference to Rome, but there is equally no necessity to place the *praitōrion* of Philippians 1:13 (see the Commentary on this verse) in Caesarea.

There are telling arguments against this proposed theory. The custody of Acts 23:35 (*cf.* 24:23) does not suggest the imminent martyrdom which Lohmeyer takes as the master theme of the entire epistle.[2] The comparative ease of his detention contrasts sharply with the 'chains' and 'struggle' of Philippians 1, and the mention of his friends hardly corresponds with Philippians 2:20–21. Hawthorne[3] calls this 'a major objection'. The size and type of Christian community at the scene of Paul's imprisonment do not favour Caesarea (1:14ff.).[4] Moreover, his outlook at the time of Acts 23–24 was bound up with a visit to Rome as we know from the Acts narrative (*cf.* 23:11) and of this desire there is no mention in Philippians. The desperate situation which confronted him, according to 1:20ff.; 2:17, could have been dispelled by an appeal to the emperor, and, in fact, this is just what happened according to Acts 25:10–12. This 'trump card', as Dodd calls it,[5] could have extricated him from danger if he were at Caesarea when his life was threatened by the authorities, and he seems to have been protected by those same

---

[1] E. Lohmeyer, *Der Brief an die Philipper* (Vandenhoeck & Ruprecht, 1929), pp. 40 f. For a critical review of Lohmeyer's commentary, *cf.* W. K. L. Clarke, *New Testament Problems* (Macmillan, 1929), pp. 141–150. *Cf.* also L. Johnson, 'The Pauline Letters from Caesarea', *ExpT*, 68, 1956, pp. 24–26.

[2] Lohmeyer, *op. cit.*, p. 3: 'Paul can count still on the possibility of release; but he seems rather to long for and await death which will bring him into eternal union with Christ.'

[3] Hawthorne, p. xliii.   [4] Bruce, *Philippians*, p. xxiii: 'Caesarea was a political backwater'.

[5] Dodd, *New Testament Studies*, p. 103.

authorities from Jewish 'conspiracy' against his life (Acts 23:12ff.). Paul's financial position, according to the witness of Acts 24:26,[1] does not seem to be in agreement with that at the time of Philippians when his 'need' is relieved only by the arrival of the gift at the hands of Epaphroditus (Phil. 4:12ff.).

3. AN EPHESIAN ORIGIN

The second possibility stems from the hypothesis that Paul suffered imprisonment at Ephesus. It is during this period of his life and against the background of the troubles which befell him 'in the province of Asia' (Acts 20:18f.; cf. 2 Cor. 1:8) that it is proposed to place the dating of Philippians, and to interpret many of the puzzling details of the letter.

At first glance the foundation of this theory seems very insecure inasmuch as the *fact* of an Ephesian imprisonment is without definite proof. Of this lack of evidence the leading exponents of the view are aware, and they freely admit that a captivity in Ephesus must remain an assumption.[2] But there is, according to these scholars, cumulative evidence which makes the hypothesis very probable, if not almost certain.

We may consider the data which are offered to support such a view as a basis for a dating of the letter.

1. The cryptic allusion in 1 Corinthians 15:32 to fighting with 'wild beasts in Ephesus'[3] may be construed either literally or metaphorically; and in either case the phrase may describe either an actual or hypothetical experience. For a figurative interpretation the statement of Ignatius (*Romans* 5) is often cited: 'From Syria to Rome I am fighting with wild beasts (*thēriomacheō* . . . bound to ten leopards, that is, a company of soldiers.'

---

[1]W. M. Ramsay, *St. Paul the Traveller and Roman Citizen* (Hodder & Stoughton,[18]1935), pp. 310 ff.

[2]Michaelis, *Einleitung*, p. 207; Collange, p. 18. It is, however, going too far to dub this lack of definite evidence a 'fatal flaw' (Hawthorne, p. xxxix) because there are several indirect pieces of data.

[3]See BAGD, *s.v. thēriomacheō.*

Ignatius quite clearly draws a distinction between the trials he endures at the hands of the soldiers who are escorting him and the expectation of his fate in the arena (5:2; *cf.* 4:1–2). In 1 Corinthians 15:32, Paul may be describing, in a vivid way, the hostility of men against him rather than his fate in which he was literally condemned *ad bestias* in the arena. Against the literal reading is also the fact that 2 Corinthians 11:23–27 fails to record it in the list of his hardships. Also his privilege as a Roman citizen would exempt him from such a punishment; but we must reckon with the possibility that, if the attack upon his life were more in the spirit of mob violence than a legal sentence of death, his plea of Roman citizenship would fall on unheeding ears as in the case of a Roman citizen who was beaten at Messina[1] or the Christian Attalus who escaped death in the amphitheatre one day when the governor knew he was a Roman, but the next day 'the governor, to please the crowd . . . delivered Attalus too again to the wild beasts'.[2]

But whether this terrifying experience were an actual fact (in which case the 'beasts' must be taken metaphorically: Paul did not die in the arena!) or relates to some event which seemed likely to happen but never did,[3] the term he uses implies some outstanding physical hardship endured at Ephesus in which there was a real threat upon his life (*cf.* 1 Cor. 15:31, 32b); and this is not the only indication there is of some danger which jeopardized the apostle's life at that time.

2. Evidence of imprisonments and severe privations prior to the Roman captivity is provided by 2 Corinthians 11:23–27, which is confirmed by the statement of Clement of Rome (5:6) that Paul 'was seven times in bonds'. Much of the Corinthian correspondence in the first and second canonical letters to the church in that place appears to reflect a great trial or series of trials he had to endure in the vicinity of Ephesus where 1 Corinthians was written. We may instance 1 Corinthians 4:9–13, and especially the sombre tones of 2 Corinthians 1:8–10 where he confesses that in (proconsular) Asia he was crushed down by

---

[1]Cicero, *in Verrem*, 5:62, 63, 66.   [2]Eusebius, *H. E.*, 5:1, 44, 50.
[3]See A. J. Malherbe, *JBL*, 87, 1968, pp. 71–80.

some fearful burden which made him despair even of life itself. 'In fact I told myself it was the sentence of death' (2 Cor. 1:9, Moffatt); but in the mercy of God he was rescued from this fate, 'so terrible a death' (v. 10, Moffatt). The same anxious mood is to be detected also in 2 Corinthians 4:8–12; 5:1–10; 6:4–10 (cf. Acts 20:18–19) written while the memory of his days at Ephesus was still vivid.[1]

With these perilous experiences Romans 16:3ff. is thought to be in close agreement. C. R. Bowen comments:[2] 'The language can scarcely mean anything else than that the apostle had been in danger of execution (cf. Rom. 16:3: "Prisca and Aquila . . . who have risked their lives for me", Moffatt) but had somehow been saved by Prisca and her husband at the hazard of their own lives.' He connects this with the exposure to the wild beasts of 1 Corinthians 15:32, whereas Dodd relates it to the troubles described in Acts 19:23–40. The former crisis may be too hypothetical for a firm identification, and the latter too mild for the language of Romans 16:3–4 (cf. 16:7: 'Andronicus and Junias . . . have been in prison with me'). All we can say is that at this period of his life at Ephesus (Romans 16 may have been written to the community there) or nearby, the apostle was in mortal peril and rescued only by divine interposition and the fearless co-operation of his friends.

3. The extra-biblical witness to an Ephesian imprisonment is admittedly of limited value. It consists of the local tradition of a watch-tower in Ephesus which is known as 'Paul's prison'; and in the 'Marcionite' Prologues, the prologue to Colossians reads: 'After he had been arrested he wrote to them (the Colossians) from Ephesus.'[3] There is also the

---

[1] See M. J. Harris, '2 Corinthians 5:1–10: Watershed in Paul's Eschatology?' *Tyndale Bulletin*, 22, 1971, pp. 32–57, for the possible effect of his Ephesian trial on Paul's outlook. A. Deissmann, *Bible Studies* (T. & T. Clark, 1901), p. 257, gives the meaning of 'the sentence of death' as an official decision of the verdict of death, but this is challenged by C. J. Hemer, 'A Note on 2 Corinthians 1:9', *Tyndale Bulletin*, 23, 1972, pp. 103–107.

[2] 'Are Paul's prison letters from Ephesus?' in *The American Journal of Theology*, 24/1, Jan. 1920, p. 116.

[3] Deissmann, *Anatolian Studies*, p. 127.

apocryphal story of Paul and the lion in the Ephesian arena.[1]

The most obvious and cogent objection against the presupposition of an imprisonment at Ephesus is *the silence of the book of Acts*. At this point, G. S. Duncan's chapter which seeks to explain the lacunae in the Acts narrative may be referred to,[2] and if his case is held to be convincing or, at least, plausible, the Ephesian dating of Philippians may be tested. Does its origin in the Ephesian period against the background of the apostle's strained predicament of those days explain or relieve the difficulties that have been earlier noted? The following are the main attractions of this novel suggestion:

1. The 'enormous journeys' between Philippi and the place of Paul's writing (which Deissmann found to be so much of an obstacle to the Roman dating) are considerably reduced. We are able to calculate with fair precision the journey time from Ephesus to Philippi. Acts 20:13ff. gives the time for the journey from Troas to Miletus as five days; to Ephesus, then, we may estimate a time of four days. Acts 16:11ff. gives three days from Troas to Philippi, and, with a contrary wind, five days (Acts 20:6). Thus the entire distance between Ephesus and Philippi would be covered in seven to nine days, and in favourable circumstances the outgoing and return journeys could be done in two weeks. So the five journeys which Deissmann regards as required by the internal evidence of the letter would be covered in not more than six weeks' travelling, and the four extra journeys which are envisaged and planned in the letter in not more than four or five weeks.

This contrasts so sharply with the lengthy distances and times required by communication between Philippi and Rome that Deissmann offers this factor as strongly supporting the Ephesian provenance of the epistle.

2. There is inscriptional evidence to satisfy the requirement of Philippians 1:13; 4:22. See these verses in the Commentary. Ephesus was the site of the proconsular headquarters, and there

---

[1]G. S. Duncan, *St. Paul's Ephesian Ministry*, pp. 69, 70 referring to one version of the tale given in R. McL. Wilson (ed.), *New Testament Apocrypha* (ET, Lutterworth, 1963), pp. 338 f.

[2]Duncan, *St. Paul's Ephesian Ministry*, ch. 9, pp. 95 ff.

would be a *praitōrion* there.[1] 'Caesar's household' may well refer to the imperial fiscal staff in that city; and there are certain advantages in this view, *e.g.* it reduces the number of praetorian guard (about 9,000 in Rome) all of whom (1:13) had heard that the apostle was a prisoner for Christ's sake.

3. At the time of Acts 19 Paul had been to Philippi only once and references to 'the early days of your acquaintance with the gospel' (4:15) read more naturally if the period between the founding of the church and the time of the letter were a short one than if it were a longer one. (So Gnilka 'it is unlikely that Paul had seen the church in the interval since its foundation'.[2]) The plans of Philippians 2 also relate with precision to the missionary itinerary of the Acts narrative: Philippians 2:19 (the mission of Timothy) will be that of Acts 19:22 (*cf.* 1 Cor. 4:17; 16:10) and Paul's hoped-for visit of 2:24 (and 1:26) will have been fulfilled in Acts 20:1 (*cf.* 19:21).

On the other hand, this neat identification has been challenged by Harrison who says that the movements of Paul following his experience of Acts 19 betray such a lack of urgency to leave Ephesus (*cf.* 1 Cor. 16:5–9) that they cannot reflect the outlook of the man who wrote of hoping 'soon' (Phil. 2:24) to revisit Philippi. But we do not know the reason for Paul's delay in Ephesus (1 Cor. 16:9), which may have been a situation which developed subsequent to his release from the imprisonment in that city and, therefore, later than the writing of Philippians. The crisis at Corinth with all its ramifications for Paul's apostolic mission may well have prompted him to defer a visit to Macedonia, especially as we do know that he did change his travel plans (2 Cor. 1:15–17, 23).

Other items of an incidental character fall into place on the assumption of an earlier dating. Acts 19:22 confirms the presence of Timothy with Paul at Ephesus, whereas there is no sure knowledge from Acts that Timothy came to Rome. Yet he was with the apostle according to Philippians 1:1.

---

[1] This is questioned by Knox, *St. Paul and the Church of the Gentiles*, pp. 178, 180; and by B. Reicke, 'Caesarea, Rome and the Captivity Letters', in *Apostolic History and the Gospel*, edd. W. W. Gasque and R. P. Martin (Paternoster/Eerdmans, 1970), pp. 277–286. See later p. 72.
[2] Gnilka, *Der Philipperbrief*, p.101.

Philippians 4:10 refers to the Philippians' desire to send help to Paul; but they had not been able to do so because they 'had no opportunity'. This can hardly have been the case if the date is some time in the years of the Roman captivity, because 4:16 will then refer to a period twelve years earlier and in that interval Paul had revisited Macedonia (Acts 20:3) and Philippi (20:6). That it must have been the first gift to the apostle that is mentioned in 4:15–16 is shown by the historical allusion to 'the early days of . . . the gospel' in 4:15. And yet Paul harks back to that time in spite of at least two visits to Philippi and recalls the lack of opportunity for further gifts! As T. W. Manson says, 'If Philippians was written from Rome, Paul's remarks on the subject of the gift sent from Philippi cannot be construed except as a rebuke, and a sarcastic rebuke at that.'[1]

If, however, only three or four years have elapsed since the first gift it will be quite true that the Philippians have had no opportunity to send a further contribution, for in that time Paul had been in the east or in the 'interior' of Acts 19:1.

To this argument Dodd raises the objection that, at the time of the Ephesian ministry, the Philippians lacked the opportunity to help because they were in the grip of a financial depression (2 Cor. 8:1–6).[2] Also he remarks upon the necessity which Paul felt, at a time when he was engaged in the task of collecting money for the Jewish 'poor' at Jerusalem, of not receiving personal gifts which may have laid him open to the charge of underhand dealings in financial matters. But the apostle never alludes to their past economic stringency to explain their tardiness to come to his help, and 4:10 suggests that they had the money in spite of their poverty but could not get it to the apostle. 2 Corinthians 8:3 records how that, even in their extreme necessity, they supported the collection 'beyond their ability'. The care with which Paul avoids the charge of covetousness (2 Cor. 12:14–19) can hardly be used as an objection to Paul's receiving the Philippians' gift in view of 4:17,

---

[1]Manson, *Studies in the Gospels and Epistles*, p. 157.
[2]Dodd, *New Testament Studies*, p. 98. See, on this and related matters, B. Holmberg, *Paul and Power* (Fortress, 1983), especially pp. 88–95.

and the objection overlooks the special bond of affection which made the church at Philippi something of a favourite in his eyes (see 4:15: 'not one church . . . except you only').

The criterion of an affinity of language and ideas with other epistles is one which we have regarded as secondary, but many scholars buttress their advocacy of an earlier dating of Philippians by a demonstration of its literary connections and theological associations with 1 and 2 Corinthians and Romans. In this way Lightfoot's linguistic parallels with Romans are justified by another route as Duncan places the two epistles to the Corinthians in close juxtaposition with Philippians immediately *before* Romans and not vice versa, as does Lightfoot.[1]

There are, nevertheless, at least two factors which militate against the proposed reconstruction of a crisis at or near Ephesus leading to Paul's arrest and mortal peril and forming the background of the hopes and fears expressed in Philippians.

1. The singular absence of any mention of the collection for the poverty-stricken Jerusalem churches is an objection which J. Schmid calls 'a chief argument' against the suggested origin of the letter.[2] We know that this matter filled Paul's thoughts and controlled many of his movements at this time (*cf.* 1 and 2 Corinthians and Romans), and yet in a letter putatively set in the context of the third missionary journey there is not a word about it.

Against this omission it is said that Timothy's mission (in Acts 19:22) which is promised in 2:19 may have been for this purpose,[3] and Paul was hopeful that he would himself soon be with them. Michael and Gnilka proffer the suggestion that instructions concerning the collection may have been given orally through Epaphroditus.

2. The second objection which has been launched against the Ephesian hypothesis is one which Schmid calls 'the decisive argument against any other dating but the Roman'.[4] In brief, the

---

[1]*Cf.* Duncan, 'Were Paul's Imprisonment Epistles written from Ephesus?', *ExpT*, 67, No. 6, March 1956, p. 164.

[2]*Zeit und Ort der paulinischen Gefangenschaftsbriefe* (Herder, 1931), p. 114.

[3]*Cf.* Harrison's discussion, *NTS*, 2, 1956, pp. 258, 259.

[4]*Zeit und Ort*, p. 107.

question is this: If Paul found himself in the hands of the authorities at Ephesus or elsewhere, why did he not exercise the right and privilege of his citizenship and appeal to Caesar[1] against any sentence of condemnation which may have been brought against him? Philippians 1:20; 2:17 reckons with an unfavourable issue of his trial (1:17) and the grim prospect of death looms large before him. If Paul was in such a desperate situation and threatened by the death sentence, why did he not do what he did at Caesarea and insist that all local proceedings be quashed and the case transferred to Rome? There are three explanations possible in answer to this question.

First, the language of 1:20 and 2:17 may be taken to describe a situation of less peril and gravity than one which would have arisen if Paul feared judicial condemnation and death. This is Michaelis' interpretation which holds that, at the time of his writing, the apostle was *not* seriously in danger because he can contemplate the possibility of both life and death in 1:20ff.; and he interprets 2:17 in a general way as referring to Paul's apostolic service in which he was daily spending his life for the gospel's sake. (Hawthorne has recently supported this view.) But a more definite danger than the hourly peril of his apostolic ministry (1 Cor. 15:31; 2 Cor. 4:10; 11:23) seems in view in the light of the cumulative weight of such verses as 1:20, 30; 2:27–28 and 3:11. 2 Timothy 4:6 which repeats the metaphor of sacrifice and offering is a later confession of a specific, serious danger to his life.[2]

Secondly, Paul may have been in danger, not from the result of formal legal procedure, but from an unofficial attempt upon his life. If the peril were from Jewish opponents (Acts 20:19) or mob violence, a protest of his Roman citizenship would be of no value, and this possibility is strengthened if the language of 1:30

---

[1] By the use of *provocatio, i.e.* a request to be tried by the emperor's court, a right which was given to Roman citizens by the *lex Iulia*, or *appellatio, i.e.* a request to obtain a revision of a judgment already given. For these technical terms in Roman law, see Sherwin-White, *Roman Society and Roman Law in the New Testament*, p.68 and in other places of his book.

[2] Dodd (*op. cit.*, p. 103, note 2) writes, 'That it is a "life and death" matter is clear from Phil. i. 20, and Paul's confidence that his life will be spared (i. 25) is not based on a calculation of probabilities, but on a conviction that his life is so important to his churches that he must escape, even though by a miracle.'

is taken literally. His present conflict (*agōn*) is the 'same' as that which he endured at Philippi (Acts 16), *viz.* a lawless outburst in which his citizenship did not save him from the lash, the stocks and the indignity of the prison.

Thirdly, Romans 16:7 speaks of Andronicus and Junia(s) as those 'in prison with me', and it has been suggested that their imprisonment with the apostle was the result of anti-Christian riots promoted by unbelieving Jews (*cf.* Acts 20:19) and that Paul did not claim his rights as a citizen because, as they were not Roman citizens, he would not leave them in the lurch.[1]

We are here in the realm of conjecture. If Paul was in danger of his life at Ephesus and for some reason refused to use his privilege to extricate himself from that peril, we can only say with Michaelis that his circumstances there are unknown to us and that, as we know too little about the courts in Ephesus, we cannot say what weight his Roman citizenship would have carried there.[2]

We come back to the traditional reading of the situation underlying the letter. The reason why he does not mention an appeal to Caesar is that just such an appeal has brought him before his judges at Rome. His grave danger is before the imperial court, and there is no more, humanly, that he can do. The threat upon his life is a very real one, but he knows that he is in God's hands; and amid the oscillation of feelings, hopes and fears reflected in the epistle (*e.g.* 2:23–24) he awaits his destiny which will be a divine opportunity for Christ to be magnified, whether by life or death (1:20).

The wheel of our investigation has, then, turned a full circle, and we are back with the possibility of a dating of the epistle in the days of the Roman imprisonment. The question must, therefore, be left as 'open'. Duncan, we feel, speaks too confidently of the Ephesian dating that 'this argument is so strong that the Ephesian origin of that letter (Philippians) ought to

---

[1]F. J. Badcock, *The Pauline Epistles* (SPCK, 1937), p. 63. But there are those who take 'fellow-prisoners' as metaphorical, meaning 'prisoners of Christ'. See C. F. D. Moule, *The Epistle to the Colossians and Philemon* (Cambridge University Press, 1957), pp. 136, 137, 140; *cf.* W.-H. Ollrog, *Paulus und seine Mitarbeiter* (Neukirchener, 1979), p.77.

[2]Michaelis, *Einleitung*, p. 209.

remain no longer a matter of dispute'.[1] The case which Duncan presents is an impressive one, but falls short of full conviction and certainty. Most scholars treat the issue as undecided but with a slight balance weighted on the side of Ephesus, with less confidence of Caesarea. Nonetheless, some such as Bruce have recently come over to the traditional location for the origin of our letter. In that state of virtual indecision,[2] it must be admitted that all sides are arguable and not one option is absolutely certain.

The choice, therefore, is between an earlier dating at the end of the winter of AD 54/55 which Michaelis proposes and with which Duncan agrees,[3] while Paul was a prisoner in or near Ephesus, or the later Roman dating in the captivity of Acts 28:30 with dates ranging from AD 61 (Kennedy) to the early part of AD 63 (Schmid).

III. AUTHENTICITY AND UNITY

By *authenticity* we are to understand the claim that the letter is a genuine production of the apostle Paul; and the clear answer may be supplied that the letter bears upon it most vividly the impress of the apostle's personality and character. There is no serious objection to its genuineness, except the section 2:5–11, on which see the Additional Note, pp. 110–114.

The attestation of Philippians in the early literature of the

---

[1] Duncan *St. Paul's Ephesian Ministry*, p. 6. A lot depends here on the placing of the Pastorals in Paul's 'mid-career', an expedient that does not please all commentators (*e.g.* Houlden, p. 42).

[2] Shared by D. Guthrie, *New Testament Introduction* (Tyndale, [3]1970), p. 535; A. H. McNeile and C. S. C. Williams, *An Introduction to the Study of the New Testament* (Oxford University Press, [2]1953), p. 183; Moule, *Colossians and Philemon*, pp. 24, 25. The closing sentence of Dibelius' commentary repeats this indecision. He concludes: 'Therefore a definite solution of this problem can hardly be reached because, even if we consider it difficult to imagine its having been composed at Rome, the Ephesian hypothesis still rests on mere supposition' (3rd edition, p. 98). But recent German scholarship (seen in Ollrog, *Paulus und seine Mitarbeiter* and G. Luedemann, *Paul, Apostle to the Gentiles*, Fortress, 1984) has taken a much more positive attitude to Paul's Ephesian trial and the close relation of Philippians to 2 Corinthians.

[3] *ExpT*, 67, 1956, p. 163; *NTS*, 5, 1958, p. 43.

Christian church is sufficient and convincing. There are indubitable echoes of the epistle in Polycarp's *Letter to the Philippians* (early second century),[1] with earlier allusions in the letters of Ignatius and 1 Clement. From that time onwards there is ample attestation in Irenaeus, Clement of Alexandria and Tertullian; and in early heretical circles.

The *unity* of the epistle is confirmed by unbroken textual tradition in which the letter is always known as a complete whole. But there are various suggestions which contest the unity of the letter mainly on the ground of an abrupt change in tone, style and content at the beginning of chapter 3. Also the sentence (3:1b): 'It is no trouble for me to write the same things to you again' has long puzzled commentators. To which 'same things' is the apostle alluding? His vitriolic attack upon the Jewish Christian schismatics of 3:2ff. and, later in the chapter, another condemnation of the 'enemies of the cross of Christ' (3:18ff.) who may be Jewish or Gentile Christians who had thrown off the constraints of the moral law (see Commentary), seem out of place in a letter of which the general tone is personal and tender. Furthermore, 3:1a, 'Finally, my brothers', looks like the conclusion of the letter whereas it is followed by two more chapters. To account for these facts two explanations are open to us.

1. INTERPOLATION

The sudden change at 3:1b is explained by the theory that these verses are really part of another Pauline letter which has somehow become interwoven into the canonical epistle. K. Lake proposed that the interpolation consisted of 3:1b – 4:3,[2] but there is no agreement among scholars as to the extent of the section which is thought to be foreign to the genuine letter. McNeile-Williams gives 3:2 – 4:1, whereas others including Bruce

---

[1]For the references *cf.* J. Moffatt, *Introduction to the Literature of the New Testament* (T. & T. Clark, [3]1918) p. 176. The texts of early witnesses to the Pauline epistles are quoted in full by A. E. Barnett, *Paul becomes a Literary Influence* (University of Chicago Press, 1941).

[2]K. Lake, *The Expositor*, 7, 1914, pp. 481–493.

think the passage ends at 4:9. There is no manuscript evidence to support such a theory which rests upon (a) the supposed incompatibility of chapter 3 with the rest of the letter and (b) the doubtful witness of Polycarp's epistle where, in 3:2, Polycarp refers to Paul who 'when he was absent wrote letters to you'.[1] Here is a mention of more than one letter sent by the apostle to the Philippian church, a fact that is very likely and understandable.[2] But that this piece of evidence confirms a partition of the canonical epistle is more debatable. This doubtfulness is shown in that Michael does not think that 3:1-19, although part of a genuine Pauline letter, was sent to the Philippians at all but 'to some correspondents whom we cannot identify'.[3]

Recent study of the letter has found several pieces of evidence which are believed to show how the extant letter as we have it is made up of several parts: (1) 3:1b seems to mark a new beginning; (2) the opponents of chapter 3 are different from the adversaries in chapter 1; (3) 4:10-23 reads like a 'Thank you' note which then comes unbelievably late in the canonical epistle, and is held to be a separate composition; and (4) Paul's

---

[1]Lightfoot, who is followed by Michaelis, Müller, and Bruce takes the plural *epistolai* (letters) as referring to a letter of importance (*cf.* Latin *litterae*) as in Eusebius, *H. E.*, VI. II. 3; 43.3. The mention in the Syrian canon (fourth century) of the *first* letter to the Philippians is usually regarded as a scribal error.

[2]On the view stated by Bauer and Harnack that the plural *epistolae* must be taken as a real plural, Bauer cites the evidence of current usage where the word refers to a number of letters, and Polycarp himself distinguishes between the singular and the plural in 13:2 of his letter. The plural then, says Bauer, means that Paul had written many times to the Philippians. Harnack argues that the plural implies that Polycarp was referring to the whole collection of Paul's letters as containing a message for particular churches.

The letters mentioned by Polycarp may include the Thessalonian letters as directed to all the churches of Macedonia, including Philippi. Harnack finds support for this in what Polycarp writes in 11:3. Here he uses the plural again and the second half of his statement, 'For concerning you he boasts in all the churches' is similar to 2 Thes. 1:4. Also in Polycarp 11:4 there seems to be a distinct allusion to 2 Thes. 3:15. This confirms Harnack's theory that Polycarp knew Paul's letters as a collection and he might, therefore, take 2 Thes. 1:3, 4 as a reference to the Philippians. This assumption has been taken a stage further by E. Schweizer who regards 2 Thessalonians as really a letter of the apostle addressed to the church at Philippi; but this theory has been justly criticized by W. Michaelis. The bibliography for this discussion may be found in W. G. Kümmel, *Introduction to the New Testament* (ET, SCM, ²1975), pp. 332-334 and Martin, *Philippians* (NCB, 1976=1980), pp. 11-13. F. F. Bruce's latest position may be read in his lecture in *BJRL*, 63, 1980-81, pp. 273-281. See further Barnett, *Paul Becomes a Literary Influence*, pp. 174, 178, 179.

[3]Michael, p. 132.

eschatological tone in 3:20–21 suggests a hope that he will survive to the parousia, as in 1 Corinthians 15:52, whereas 1:23 with its realistic prospect of having to die is akin to 2 Corinthians 5:1–10 and developed later in his thought. So Philippians 3 antedates chapter 1.[1]

But each of these items is open to another viewpoint which the present writer has dealt with at some length elsewhere.[2] Briefly, it may be said: (1) 3:1b can very well be understood as looking ahead to the warnings and directives mentioned later in chapter 3 as part of the visits of Timothy and Epaphroditus (2:23, 28–29); (2) the opponents in 1:27 – 2:18 and 3:18ff. are by no means identical, and so Paul's attitude to them may well be different. But even if Paul *is* facing one main opposing or heretical tendency at Philippi (as is likely), it is still by no means certain that we should have to posit two separate life-settings for chapters 1–2 and 3; (3) we will submit that already in 1:3, 5 Paul is acknowledging the generosity of his readers in their gifts to him; and (4) any attempt to trace a drastic shift in Paul's eschatology from 1 Corinthians to 2 Corinthians or within this letter is open to objection. Added to this reply we must call attention to the positive evidence of the strong links in both language and concepts that bind the letter into a unity, and question how a final editor reasoned when he (hypothetically) assembled the letter in the order in which the verses now stand.[3]

2. INTERRUPTION

The sudden change in style and outlook may be accounted for by an interruption in the apostle's dictation which brought him news either of some event at the place of his imprisonment or (more likely) news of some new disturbance at Philippi which led him to write a detailed warning against the enemies of the

[1]See Bruce, *BJRL*, 63, 1980–81, pp. 279–280 for a tentative response to this.
[2]Martin, *Philippians* (NCB, 1976=1980), pp. 14–22.
[3]See Kümmel, *Introduction*, p. 334; Guthrie, *New Testament Introduction*, pp. 536–539; Hawthorne, pp. xxix–xxxii.

gospel. In either case it appears that the occasion of the sharp-toned warning was the activity and danger of the Jewish gnosticizing teachers[1] whom we may recognize in chapter 3. This diversion and full-length treatment of a newly apparent situation here, which was created by the arrival of distressing news, is reflected in his style as the tempo of his dictation becomes brisker and words are repeated (cf. 3:2, 7–9). A retracing of his thoughts and words as though he wishes to explain them more fully has been noted also. All this betrays the mind of an agitated and deeply-moved thinker who was confronted with a situation on which he could only express himself with feeling and deep concern for the truth of God and the safety of his beloved church at Philippi.

'Finally, my brothers, rejoice in the Lord!' (3:1a), then, is the intended conclusion of the letter. Paul is interrupted by stirring news and quickly turns aside to dictate a vehement warning. 'The same things' is a prospective term, looking forward to the serious admonitions to watchfulness against the sectarians which are to follow. Possibly the apostle may have written in an earlier letter which is no longer extant about the perils of this movement, and have set his readers on their mettle against his bitter opponents and detractors especially if 2 Corinthians 10–13 belongs to the same period of his life. Note the evidence of 2 Corinthians 7:5: 'For when we came into Macedonia, this body of ours had no rest, but we were harassed at every turn— conflicts on the outside, fears within.' Has he just heard of their renewed activity at Philippi and finds it needful to repeat former warnings for the safety of the church? This long treatment extends up to and closes on the note of 4:1 with a reiterated call to steadfastness in the Lord against any spiritual danger from this direction.

[1]For a more precise formulation of this sectarian influence, see my *Philippians* (NCB, 1976=1980), pp. 22–36.

IV. OCCASION AND PURPOSE

The apostle's situation as a prisoner and his plans for the future, if, in the mercy of God, he was released, have already been mentioned (see pp. 21–25). The proposals to send his colleagues, Timothy and Epaphroditus, have also been referred to in the section in which the number of journeys to and from the scene of his captivity was discussed. In the sending back of Epaphroditus to his native Philippi (2:25ff.) we may see the immediate occasion of the letter; and in Paul's desire to commend this Christian colleague to his fellow-believers at Philippi, and to disarm any criticism which may have been levelled against him (see the Commentary on these verses), we may find the most obvious purpose which prompted the writing of the epistle. E. F. Scott names this desire to ensure a good reception for Epaphroditus as the main aim of Philippians.[1] There are, however, other reasons for the composition of the letter, apart from the reassurance that the apostle was in good heart, although in prison, and the necessity of Epaphroditus' return.

1. In 1:3, 5; 4:10, 14ff. Paul pays warm tribute to the repeated generosity of the church in the material help which it had sent to him. In spite of their poverty-stricken condition (2 Cor. 8:1ff.) they had assisted the ministry of the apostle right from the time when he left Philippi after the first visit (1:5, 4:15). At Thessalonica (4:16), and at Corinth (2 Cor. 11:9) gifts had reached him; and, as a crowning gesture, the church had commissioned its member Epaphroditus to become its 'messenger', and 'to take care' of Paul's needs (2:25) both by the further gift which came by his hands (4:18), and by the ministry of companionship and succour which he was able to exercise at the apostle's side (2:25, 30).

These fine actions Paul would gratefully acknowledge. He singles out the 'overseers' and deacons' (1:1) in the opening salutation because most probably they were instrumental in collecting the money which formed the gift received through

---

[1] Scott, p. 10.

Epaphroditus.[1] He expresses his gratitude by the use of exalted language which shows that he appreciated the gifts not only as a service rendered to him personally, but as a contribution to the work of God and the gospel. The gestures and gifts of the Philippians are invested with special significance as setting forth the apostolic ministry. Thus, their 'partnership' (1:5) with him is 'in the gospel'. Epaphroditus 'ministered' (2:25, RSV) – a word with solemn and sacred associations of some work undertaken for religious purposes.[2]

2. Epaphroditus, it is clear, came also with news of the outbreak of various troubles at Philippi. The most obvious defect to mar the church's fair reputation was its disunity. That there were differences of opinion and internal disturbances within the assembly is clear from 2:2–4, 14; 4:2 and possibly 1:27. The frequent use of the word 'all' (1:1, 4, 7 [twice], 8, 25; 2:26; 4:21), which Lightfoot calls 'a studied repetition', is connected with the apostle's appeal for unity and concord. This reiterated inclusion of all the members would be both a reminder to them of the wrongness of their divisions and quarrelsomeness, and a quiet and effective dispelling of any notion that some of them may have entertained that they were outside the circle of his favour. Then there is the highest summons to self-forgetting humility in 2:5–11 setting out the true understanding of their calling 'in Christ' as members of his church and reminding them of a disposition and standard of behaviour which this privilege imposes upon them.

Another source of confusion seems to have been a 'perfectionist' wing within the church. Although such a group of Christians who believed that they had 'arrived' spiritually and were complacently perfect is not explicitly mentioned, Paul does expressly mention some who are 'thinking differently' (3:15) after his personal disclaimer to have attained the perfection towards which he is continually pressing forward. Scott's estimate is a fair inference: 'It can hardly be doubted that Paul

---

[1]Michaelis, *Einleitung*, p. 202. But against this there is no mention of them in 4:10–20.

[2]W. Barclay, *A New Testament Wordbook* (SCM, 1955), pp. 74–76; more recently incorporated into *New Testament Words* (Westminster, 1974), pp. 176–178.

here (in chapter 3) deals with a question which was warmly debated in the Philippian church.'[1] Recent studies have more precisely seen here a type of faulty eschatology which imagined that, since believers have been raised in Christ to new life, this was their final salvation in its fullness. Such a 'realized eschatology' would breed false claims for present perfection, promising exemption from suffering, and leading to a denial of a future resurrection. These three traits suggest a species of what later became fully blown gnosticism, *i.e.* a religious attitude to life now, based on special knowledge (*gnōsis*).

A further warning is directed against faintheartedness in time of trial. Certain references in 1:27–30; 2:15; 4:1 contain hints that the infant church at Philippi, set in a pagan world and with the dangers of the false teaching of Jewish gnostics looming on the horizon, was quailing before the opposition which confronted it. The letter is a document of exhortation in which the apostle, himself facing the severe trial of impending martyrdom, rallies his beloved Philippians to share steadfastly with him the fellowship of Christ's sufferings (3:10–11), and to remain true and loyal in the face of their adversaries. The key term is 'knowledge' (*gnōsis*) in 3:8, 10, a term much prized by the false teachers, and now 'disinfected' and used against them. Paul too vindicates his role as suffering apostle.

Lohmeyer, however, carries this evidence to an extreme in his exposition of the epistle entirely in terms of martyrdom. On this view, which has not been followed with scholarly agreement, Paul the martyr is appealing to a persecuted community at Philippi, and this is the *leitmotiv* of the whole letter. While there is evidence that the believers addressed in the letter were undergoing a conflict for their faith (1:29–30), some of the additional evidence which Lohmeyer deduces is questionable. For example, the suggestion that 'joy' in Philippians always denotes 'rejoicing in martyrdom'[2] unduly narrows the scope of the word in many places.[3]

---

[1]Scott p. 11.   [2]Lohmeyer, p. 16, note 3.
[3]See, for a criticism, W. K. Lowther Clarke, *New Testament Problems* (Macmillan, 1929), pp. 142, 143.

The change of style and subject-matter at 3:1b is noticeable to all readers, and has called forth various explanations.[1] Assuming that what follows in chapter 3 is in the nature of a digression as Paul receives news of the operation of Jewish sectarians (see above pp. 40–41), this chapter may be reckoned as providing another reason for the letter. While the threats are couched in the language of what seems only an imminent danger, it is clear that the Philippian church was succumbing to wrong-headed ideas. Hence Paul's warnings are pointed and realistic (*e.g.* 3:2).

V. FEATURES OF THE LETTER

'The Apostle and his Friends' is the New English Bible's caption to sum up the message of Philippians. This impression of intimacy and cordiality is re-echoed by all commentators, and forms the most noticeable characteristic which distinguishes Philippians in the Pauline literature. The word 'joy' in its verbal and noun forms is found sixteen times in the four chapters of the letter. Bengel's well-known comment, then, is fully justified: *summa epistolae; gaudeo, gaudete*:[2] 'the content of the letter; I rejoice, (now) you rejoice!'

The value of this fact lies surely in its clear indication that Paul was enabled to rejoice in the most trying circumstances of his captivity. The example of a man whose life is filled with joy, and his exhortations to 'rejoice in the Lord', do not proceed from some ivory tower of peace and security. On the contrary, the writer is Paul the prisoner, who is awaiting news which may spell his death; and one can, with a little sympathetic imagination, share the tension behind such verses as 1:20, 22–23; 2:17; 3:10–11.

Joy as a fruit of the Spirit (Gal. 5:22) is no evanescent emotional quality, exalting us one moment and deserting us the next. For the apostle is never the victim of despair and depression in spite of his outward situation. He knows, from bitter

---

[1] See pp. 38–41 above.   [2] J. A. Bengel on 1:4.

experience, what it means to be abased (4:12) but he is never utterly in hopeless despair (see 2 Cor. 4:8–10); and he shares his secret in this letter.

Chapter 4:6 offers the injunction, 'Do not be anxious', and we may be sure that the apostle availed himself of his own secret of inward peace and tranquillity by the resources of 'prayer and petition'. By these means he knew the peace of God in his heart and the joy of the Lord as his perpetual strength.

Furthermore, the reason for his 'radiance amid the storm and stress of life' – a phrase of von Hügel's which might well epitomize the apostle's outlook as reflected in the letter – is clearly given as his living union with Christ. 'For to me, to live is Christ and to die is gain' (1:21) is a statement which reveals how the soul is nurtured and protected in adversity, and the prospect for the future, quite irrespective of what happens to the body (1:20), maintained. This hope for the future, moreover, is inspired by the promise of the Lord's return in glory which runs like a thread through the epistle (see 1:6, 10; 2:11; 3:20–21; 4:5).

Paul's great ambition is to enter more deeply into communion with Christ (3:10); but this is no self-centred mystical piety after the fashion of the Hellenistic mystery-cults (as Dibelius thinks[1]). He cannot forget the welfare of others (1:24–27); and part of his joy is fulfilled in the prayer he offers on their behalf (1:4, 9–10), and in the expectation that they will do as he enjoins (2:2). He finds joy in the Lord not only in exalted spiritual experience (2:17) and the life of communion and prayer, but in mundane events which faith invests with spiritual significance. Notable is the arrival of Epaphroditus who came with the Philippians' gift (2:25; 4:10); and Paul will find gladness in the confidence that Epaphroditus will be heartily welcomed back (2:28).

The apostle can lift up his heart in rejoicing both under the shadow of impending martyrdom and in the kindly light of Christian generosity because, above all, he is rejoicing not in these things primarily but 'in the Lord' himself (3:1; 4:4).

The thought leads on to a consideration of the pervasive supremacy of the person of the Lord Jesus Christ throughout

[1]M. Dibelius, at 3:8, p. 89.

the letter. It is no exaggeration to say that this epistle is 'full of Christ', commencing with the remarkable frequency of the divine names in the opening verses ('Christ Jesus' [twice] in verse 1; 'the Lord Jesus Christ' in verse 2) and closing with a prayer for the grace of 'the Lord Jesus Christ' where the full New Testament title (in Paul's writings) gives a profound impression. Paul might well have expressed his conviction in Wesley's words:

> My heart is full of Christ, and longs
> Its glorious matter to declare!

The *locus classicus* of Pauline Christological doctrine is 2:5–11 with its deep teaching on the pre-existent, incarnate and exalted states of Christ in a hymn which J. Jeremias regards as 'the oldest evidence for the teaching concerning the three states of Christ's existence which underlies and delimits the entire christology of later times'.[1]

But it is also in the incidental allusions to the Lord's person that his central place in the life of the believer and the church is found. The important phrase 'in Christ' (or 'in the Lord', 'in him') is a frequently used formula in these chapters. Exhortation is 'in Christ' (2:1, RSV). Paul rejoices 'in the Lord' (4:10), and calls upon his readers to do the same (3:1; 4:4). He hopes 'in the Lord Jesus' (2:19) when making future plans. The anticipation of his release and re-visit to Philippi is controlled by the thought, 'in the Lord' (2:24). If he is released and able to renew contact with the church it will be an occasion of 'joy in Christ Jesus . . . (to) overflow' (1:26). Power for effective service is found only 'in him' (4:13, RSV). Likewise the believer's steadfastness is secured only as he stands fast 'in the Lord' (4:1).

Epaphroditus is to be received, not simply with cordiality and friendliness, but 'in the Lord' (see Commentary on 2:29). Paul's imprisonment is 'in Christ', *i.e.* he is a prisoner because of his

---

[1] J. Jeremias, 'Zur Gedankenführung in den paulinischen Briefen.' in *Studia Paulina in honorem de Zwaan*, edd. by J. N. Sevenster and W. C. van Unnik (Bohn, 1953), p. 154. This conclusion is still defensible in spite of recent challenges from either those who treat the passage as referring to the earthly Jesus or those who are disposed to deny the element of pre-existence in 2:6. For such a defence, see the relevant essays in *Christ the Lord. Studies in Christology presented to Donald Guthrie*, ed. H. H. Rowdon (IVP, 1982).

loyalty to him (1:13, see NEB). In 2:5 the attitude which is to be the ruling pattern of Christian conduct is such as would be found 'in Christ Jesus', *i.e.* as members of his church (*cf.* RSV).[1]

Paul's own confession, 'For to me, to live is Christ' (1:21) receives no clearer substantiation than in the evidence set out above. Every part of his thought and life was directly related to the one who had taken hold of him (3:12) and whom it was his supreme ideal and aim to know and to make known, so that at the last day he might be 'found in him', justified by his righteousness and receiving the prize of the upward call of God in him unto the glory and praise of God (1:8–11).

Two remaining terms demand our attention as we consider the linguistic usages of the epistle. One study in Pauline language makes the interesting observation that the apostle not infrequently sums up the argument or the standpoint of a given epistle in one outstanding term or phrase.[2] It suggests 'the righteousness of God' for Romans, 'the fullness' for Colossians and 'the heavenly places' for Ephesians. While this is an oversimplification of Pauline literary themes, we may ask what phrase or phrases sum up Philippians. Two suggestions may be offered.

1. Fellowship, *koinōnia*, is a rich New Testament word, the precise meaning of which has received a great deal of attentive study in recent years.[3] Basically it denotes 'participation in something with someone'; and its meaning that Christians share with one another in a common possession (for example, 'the gospel' in 1:5; 'the Spirit' in 2:1) is far more important than the popular modern idea of a personal association with fellow-Christians as when we use the word of a friendly atmosphere in a public meeting.

---

[1]For this meaning see the commentary at 2:5. *Cf.* R. Bultmann, *Theology of the New Testament*, 1 (ET, SCM, 1952), p. 311: ' "In Christ", far from being a formula for mystic union, is primarily an *ecclesiological* formula.'

[2]R. M. Pope, *Studies in the Language of St. Paul* (Epworth, 1936), p. 110.

[3]See the present author's contribution to *IBD* part 1, under 'Communion' for bibliography to which should be added: P. T. O'Brien, 'The Fellowship Theme in Philippians', *Reformed Theological Review*, 37, 1978, pp. 9–18; G. Panikulam, *Koinōnia in the New Testament* (Pontifical Biblical Institute, 1979); J. Hainz, *Koinonia. 'Kirche' als Gemeinschaft bei Paulus*, Biblische Untersuchungen 16 (Fr. Pustet, 1982).

In this latter sense of a bond joining Christians together it is never found in Paul, according to Lohmeyer. Its usual meaning is one of participation in an object outside of subjective experience, an 'objective work' as Lohmeyer calls it.[1]

The precise definition of *koinōnia* in any text will vary with the context. In certain cases (*e.g.* Rom. 15:26; 2 Cor. 9:13), the meaning is that of generosity, but not in an abstract sense. It is a generosity which shows itself in the tangible and realistic expression of giving, and so the word comes to mean a financial contribution (as clearly in Rom. 15:26).

The idea underlying *koinōnia* is found in the following references in Philippians: 1:5, 7; 2:1; 3:10; 4:14–15. Of these references the most important theologically are:

a. 1:5: 'your partnership (*koinōnia*) in the gospel'. The word here expresses the object of Paul's thanks to God. But what is the precise sense of this object? It is hard to believe that the apostle makes no reference to the practical help which the Philippians had given him 'from the first day', which appears to mean the same as 'in the early days of your acquaintance with the gospel' (4:15). They had continued to show their interest in the gospel by their repeated contributions. Thus the meaning here is 'your co-operation towards, in aid of the Gospel' (so Lightfoot). This usage of the preposition *eis*, translated here 'in', is confirmed in the papyri where it denotes the object in respect of which money is paid in the items of an account.[2] The Philippians indicated the reality of their partnership in the gospel not by 'a quiet enjoyment of it, but (by) a keen activity in the interest of it'.[3]

But we need not restrict the meaning here exclusively to the monetary support of the church. In 2 Corinthians 9:13 the translation 'generosity' best fits the context, and we may propose it for the present verse. As a Christian virtue generosity was a hallmark of the Philippian believers, and the apostle is praising

[1]Lohmeyer, p. 17. *Cf.* Lake and Jackson, *The Beginnings of Christianity*, 5 (2), 1933, p. 390. But this needs to be qualified by what he says on 3:10 (pp. 138, 139) where the genitive following *koinōnia*, if it denotes a religious possession, provides the foundation and norm by means of which fellowship is made possible and practical.
[2]Moulton-Milligan, pp. 186, 187.   [3]J. Müller, p.40.

God for his work of grace in the lives of his people who have shown the genuineness of their faith by their gifts (2 Cor. 8:1–2).

H. Seesemann[1] sees no reference to the church's gift in this verse, and takes 'fellowship' as equivalent to their faith in Christ which the preaching of the gospel produced on the first day, *i.e.* the day of their conversion. But with Paul it is ever the case that 'faith expresses itself through love' (see Gal. 5:6); and love must ever be embodied in action. Hence the two main interpretations of *koinōnia* here fuse together.

b. 2:1: literally rendered as 'any fellowship (*koinōnia*) of the Spirit (*pneumatos*)'. The main issue in interpreting this phrase is whether the genitive, 'of the Spirit', is subjective or objective, *i.e.* whether it is to be rendered 'fellowship created by the Holy Spirit, fellowship which he makes possible'[2] or 'fellowship in the Holy Spirit' which comes about through the believer's possession of him.

The detailed discussions of Seesemann and A. R. George may be consulted for fuller information;[3] but we may summarize Seesemann's convincing argument for the view that the genitive here must be objective, and the phrase translated with NIV, 'fellowship with the Spirit', or in RSV as 'any participation in the Spirit'.

He notes that the apostle takes the possession of the Holy Spirit by the believer as a truth readily acknowledged and experienced by his readers, as in Galatians 3:2. Also, there is a parallel in 1 Corinthians 1:9 where the meaning is 'participation in Christ';[4] and there is evidence from writers in the early church that the phrase *koinōnia pneumatos* is taken by them to mean 'participation in the Spirit'. Finally, Seesemann bases an

---

[1]H. Seesemann, *Der Begriff Koinōnia im N.T.*, BZNTW 14 (Töpelmann, 1933), pp. 74, 75, 76. But Hainz (*Koinōnia*, pp. 93–95) is critical of this understanding for which Seesemann quotes Theodoret 'fellowship in the Gospel is what Paul calls "faith" '. Hainz prefers Lohmeyer's view that Paul is referring to his apostolic work.

[2]This thought is elsewhere expressed in Paul's letters as 'the unity of the Spirit' (Eph. 4:3).

[3]Seesemann, *Der Begriff Koinōnia*, pp. 56–62, and following Seesemann, A. R. George, *Communion with God in the New Testament* (Epworth, 1953), p. 178.

[4]See George, *ibid.*, pp. 175–177. But 2 Corinthians 13:14 is appealed to by Hawthorne to argue for 'fellowship created by the Holy Spirit' – a doubtful interpretation, however; see further, Hainz, *Koinōnia*, pp. 51–55.

argument on the form of Paul's wording in the verse by taking the four phrases of the apostle's appeal as two sets of pairs. 'The fellowship of the Spirit' and 'affection and sympathy' (RSV) go together as something interior to the Christian over against 'encouragement' and 'comfort' which are external to him. To take the genitive *pneumatos*, 'of the Spirit', as subjective here would ruin the parallelism because it would imply an action outside the believer's experience rather than a subjective experience, his 'share in the Spirit', which, like 'heartfelt sympathy', is an internal quality of his life.

The case which is outlined above seems to be convincing, and 'participation in the Spirit' is the best translation.

c. 3:10: 'the fellowship of . . . his sufferings'. Again the debate turns on the definition of the genitive, *pathēmatōn autou*, 'his sufferings'. It is generally agreed that the genitive must be objective, with the idea that Paul shares in his Lord's sufferings (so NIV, RSV) rather than 'the fellowship created by his sufferings'.[1] Lohmeyer, however, takes it in this latter sense with the comment that 'his sufferings are the foundation of the fellowship of the believer with Christ or God'.[2] But, as Seesemann observes, 'with Christ or God' is an addition which is unwarranted by the context.

The drift of the sentence is clear, even if the thought is breathtaking. The apostle longs to know Christ in such a personal and intimate way that he may enter into the deep experience of his resurrection and sufferings. The order of words is unusual. Why is the resurrection mentioned *before* the cross? This can only be satisfactorily explained by remembering that, in the apostle's thought, when Christ was raised from the dead, his people shared in that resurrection, and rose in him to newness of life (Rom. 6:4; Col. 3:1, 3). Therefore it is only as we know that new life, which is his risen life, within us by our union in faith that we enter into the depths of his sufferings.[3]

---

[1]Seesemann, *Der Begriff Koinōnia*, pp. 83–86; George, *Communion with God*, pp. 183, 184; Hainz, *Koinōnia*, pp. 95–99.

[2]Lohmeyer, p. 139.

[3]The literature of Pauline teaching of dying, rising and living with Christ is immense. *Cf.* R. C. Tannehill, *Dying and Rising with Christ*, BZNTW 32 (Töpelmann, 1967).

'Sharing in his sufferings' is a phrase which needs to be interpreted carefully. We cannot say that the apostle's hard lot or privation and persecution adds anything redemptively to the pains endured at Calvary. The work of atonement there was complete and final. On the other hand, we must not evacuate this phrase of its rich meaning by taking it to mean simply that he shared his Lord's sufferings in imagination or sympathy or that he suffered only for his sake or 'with him' in a general sense.

The thought of a spiritual union with Christ in his death and resurrection, which is at the very heart of Paul's experience and teaching, is the key here. So close is this intimacy of knowledge and experience with his Lord that he can regard his apostolic career as an inner participation in his sufferings, which has almost the character of identity.[1] But the identity is never complete, although it is elsewhere forcefully expressed (*e.g.* 2 Cor. 4:10) as a 'bearing about in the body the dying of the Lord Jesus'. But there is no confusion which might suggest a 'mystical absorption' with Christ or detract from the unique finality of the Saviour's work at Calvary.

2. A second characteristic term of the letter is 'gospel'.[2] It is found seven times (1:5, 7, 12, 27; 2:22; 4:3, 15). Except in 1:27 the meaning is uniformly the same. It denotes the apostolic ministry and work of evangelization which God entrusted into Paul's hands. He is assisted in this task of 'the gospel of the uncircumcision', *i.e.* an evangelistic mission to non-Jews (Gal. 2:7), by the companionship of Timothy (2:22) and others, including womenfolk (4:3). The Philippians have helped, at a distance, by their regular gifts and 'fellowship' (1:5) since the day when Paul first visited their city with the good news of Christ's redemption (4:15). For the sake of the gospel Paul is a prisoner

---

[1] Seesemann, *Der Begriff Koinōnia*, p. 86. See B. M. Ahern, ' "The Fellowship of His Sufferings" (Phil. 3, 10)', *CBQ*, 22, 1960, pp. 1–32.

[2] See, for the background of this term, G. N. Stanton, *Jesus of Nazareth in New Testament Preaching*, SNTSMS 27 (Cambridge University Press, 1967); J. A. Fitzmyer, 'The Gospel in the Theology of Paul' in *Interpreting the Gospels*, ed. J. L. Mays (Fortress Press, 1981), pp. 1–13; and for a survey on the New Testament reference to 'Gospel', see R. P. Martin, 'Gospel', *International Standard Bible Encyclopedia*, 2, eds. G. W. Bromiley, *et al.* (Eerdmans, 1982), pp. 529–532.

(1:13, 17), yet he rejoices that, although he is in captivity, the Word of God is not bound because God is inspiring fresh voices to herald the message of Christ (1:18) and so to speed the gospel which he was charged to deliver to the nations on its triumphant way (1:12; *cf.* 2 Thes. 3:1).

Of special interest is the description in 4:15: 'as you Philippians know, in the early days of your acquaintance with the gospel . . .' (NIV, which is a paraphrase here). The text of the letter says only 'in the beginning of the gospel', referring back to Paul's first mission preaching in Philippi (1:6; Acts 16:12ff.). The term 'gospel' takes on a personal significance, well brought out in NIV.[1] But more significantly perhaps this verse shows how Paul regarded the strategic importance of his coming to Philippi and the opening of his mission in Macedonia which may justifiably be called a 'decisive turning-point'. Thereafter Macedonia – and Philippi in particular – remained in the foreground of Paul's mission endeavour, his commitment to the 'gospel'.

---

[1] See P. T. O'Brien, 'Thanksgiving and the Gospel in Paul', *NTS*, 21, 1975, pp. 144–155, esp. pp. 153 f.

ANALYSIS

I. ADDRESS AND SALUTATION (1:1–2)

II. PAUL'S THANKSGIVING AND CONFIDENCE (1:3–7)

III. AN APOSTOLIC PRAYER (1:8–11)

IV. PAUL'S GREAT AMBITION AND JOY (1:12–26)
    a. Unexpected results of his imprisonment (1:12–14)
    b. Motives – sincere and mixed (1:15–18)
    c. Paul's dilemma, and confidence, in life and death (1:19–26)

V. EXHORTATIONS TO THE COMMUNITY (1:27 – 2:18)
    a. Exhortation to unity and courage in the face of alien influences (1:27–30)
    b. Exhortation to harmony and humility in the face of factiousness (2:1–4)
    c. The 'Way' of Christ (2:5–11)
    d. Exhortation applied, and the example of Paul (2:12–18)

VI. FUTURE PLANS (2:19–30)
    a. The commendation of Timothy (2:19–24)
    b. The commendation of Epaphroditus (2:25–30)

VII. WARNINGS AND ENCOURAGEMENTS (3:1–21)
    a. Paul's warning and claim (3:1–3)
    b. Paul's autobiography (3:4–14)
        i. His Jewish inheritance (3:4–6)

COMMENTARY

I. ADDRESS AND SALUTATION (1:1–2)

1. The apostle opens his letter in the conventional way, according to the pattern of ancient letter-writing which we know from the Jewish literature of both Old Testament (Ezr. 7:12; Dn. 4:1) and later writings (2 Baruch 78:2), as well as the surviving papyri. The opening words usually take the form of the names of the writer and recipient and a greeting (*cf.* Acts 23:25–26).[1] It is the specifically Christian features in Paul's epistles which are important; and in these opening verses a remarkable touch is the frequency with which the divine names are mentioned. The apostle declares unmistakably his Christian faith which is centred in the persons of Godhead.

Another exceptional feature is the description of Paul and Timothy as *servants of Christ Jesus*. Timothy's name appears in view of his association with the apostle in his imprisonment, and also because of his special connection with the Philippians (see notes on 2:19–24). There is no hint that the apostle's junior colleague had any share in the writing of the letter. The reason for the mention of Timothy is more likely to be found in the apostle's thankfulness that, in his time of need, he could count upon the steadfast loyalty of his 'son in the faith' (*cf.* 2:22); and he joins Timothy's name to his own as a mark of esteem (*cf.* 'my fellow-worker', Rom. 16:21), and also to pave the way for his announcement of his future plans in chapter 2.

[1] See W. G. Doty, *Letters in Primitive Christianity* (Fortress Press, 1973), pp. 21–33.

Both men are called *servants*, lit. 'slaves', *of Christ Jesus*. Deiss-mann traces this title to the Hellenistic custom of manumission in which the slave was set free by a money payment, and thereby became a devotee of the deity.[1] This setting for Paul's self-designation is supported by Bruce, Getty, and Hawthorne who see a link between Christian leaders as 'slaves' and the example of humble service given in 2:6–8. It is more probable, however, that in this context the Pauline expression goes back to the Old Testament. In its Hebrew form, *'ebed Yahweh*, the phrase is used of Moses (Ex. 14:31; Nu. 12:7; Ps. 105:26) and the proph-ets (Je. 25:4; Dn. 9:6,10; Am. 3:7) to denote their God-given authority as the accredited messengers of the Lord. It was, therefore, a title of dignity. 'To be a servant, in the religious language of Judaism, meant to be one chosen by God' (Loh-meyer, on 2:7). The title emphasizes not servitude but instru-mentality, that is, God is pleased to work through his servants. Thus, though Paul makes no explicit claim to apostleship in the opening of the letter (probably because his office as an apostle had not been challenged at Philippi and there was a special bond of affection between him and the believers there), in this phrase we may catch the undertone of his authority. Timothy shares the dignity of the title because he will be shortly coming to Philippi (2:23; *cf.* Acts 19:22) in Paul's name, and as the apostle's special envoy.

The epistle is a warm-hearted, pastoral letter but the note of apostolic authority equally runs throughout it. Right at the beginning Paul is making clear that he is addressing his readers in the full consciousness of his position as an apostle, invested with God-given authority (2 Cor. 10:8), yet based on service to the highest authority of all. This high conception of the apostolic status of Paul endorses J. Gresham Machen's important observation that 'everywhere in the Epistles . . . the attitude of Paul toward Christ is not merely the attitude of man to man, or scholar to master; it is the attitude of man toward God'.[2] The men of God in the Old Testament derived their authority from

---

[1] A. Deissmann, *Light from the Ancient East* (Hodder and Stoughton, ⁴1927), p. 322.
[2] J. Gresham Machen, *The Origin of Paul's Religion* (Eerdmans, 1947), p. 198.

Yahweh. Paul, in the same honoured succession, traces back his high calling to *Christ Jesus*, a sure token of his awareness of the Lord's divine nature.

To all the saints in Christ Jesus at Philippi, is a comprehensive phrase to describe the Christian community which had been formed following the apostolic mission at Philippi (Acts 16:12ff., on which see the Introduction).

Saints, hagioi, is a term which is found only in the plural in the New Testament, except in 4:21 where, however, the word refers to a group. It is applied to all New Testament Christians, not to a select body of spiritual elite. *Hagios* means 'holy', equivalent in the Old Testament to a Hebrew word meaning 'to separate'. The saints are the separated ones in a double sense; negatively, there is separation from evil, and positively, dedication to God and his service. In the Old Testament, Israel is God's holy people in precisely these two ways. It is a nation separated from the rest of the ancient world (Nu. 23:9; Ps. 147:20) by divine election and calling; and its national life is distinctive as a witness to God because it is called to be 'a holy nation' (Ex. 19:5–6; Lv. 19:1–2; Dt. 7:6; 14:2). The church is the successor to the sacred community of Israel (see 1 Pet. 2:9–10), and the ancient call of God to his people, 'Be holy', is renewed to those who are *in Christ Jesus*, to be his people in the days when God's eschatological purposes are being fulfilled in the creation of 'the saints of the Most High' (Dn.7:18, 22, 27).

The Christians' calling to a life of 'sainthood', *i.e.* holiness, is *in Christ Jesus*. Only by our faith-union with Christ in his death and resurrection can this life become a reality. As Barth expresses it: 'Their holiness is and remains in Christ Jesus. It is in Him they are holy. It is from this point of view that they are to be addressed as such, in no other respect' (*cf.* 1 Cor. 1:30).

Paul singles out for special mention *the overseers and deacons*. These terms, *episkopoi, diakonoi*, were taken over from contemporary society as well as the religious language of the Old Testament where the twin ideas are oversight and service. In early Christian writing, however, the terms refer to the inner life of the church as an organized fellowship. Some commentators (Gnilka, Hawthorne) argue that the terms describe the holders of ecclesiastical office however rudimentary. Others think more of church leaders who exercised a specific responsibility which was assumed by certain Christians in the local church. There is no definite article in the Greek, and it is noteworthy that there were *overseers* (in the plural) in the Philippian church.

The duty of the *episkopos* in the earlier Pauline churches is clearly set out in Acts 20:28. The word is there translated 'overseers' and it is clear that the persons so referred to are those who, in Acts 20:17, are called 'elders of the church'. The responsibility of such leaders is that of nourishing and protecting the 'flock of God'. In the church at Philippi there were a number of such *episkopoi* drawn from the rank and file of the church, and although these persons are specially mentioned in the opening salutation, they are not given any prominence in the body of the letter nor are they referred to at 4:10–20 where Paul expresses his thanks for the Philippians' gifts. The apostle writes to a whole church, and there is no suggestion of a small group which held ecclesiastical office as in the later 1 Clement 42. The work of an 'overseer' is mentioned in the documents of the Qumran sect, notably in the *Rule of the Community*.

The *diakonoi* took their name from those who, in the secular world, were responsible for certain welfare duties in the community (*e.g.* the distribution of gifts and food). The Christian deacon, whose origin is usually traced to the ministry of the Seven in Acts 6, though the actual title 'deacon' does not appear there, may be regarded as a person who had certain administrative tasks in the church; but here again no definite office is in view. B. S. Easton quotes 1 Corinthians 12:28 ('able to help others . . . administration') and 16:15–16 ('the *diakonia* of the saints') as a rough parallel to the function of the Philippian deacons.[1]

It is possible but not provable that these persons are specially referred to in the opening address because they had taken the initiative in collecting and sending the gift of the church by the

---

[1] B. S. Easton, *The Pastoral Epistles* (SCM, 1948), pp. 224, 225. See too H. von Campenhausen, *Ecclesiastical Authority and Spiritual Power in the Church of the First Three Centuries* (ET, A. & C. Black, 1968).

hands of Epaphroditus (2:25; 4:18), and the financial work of bishops and deacons is later attested in the Pastoral Epistles. Hawthorne has suggested that, with the translation 'the overseers who serve', only one group is in view. This suggestion enables him to give a reason for the mention of these leaders at the head of Paul's letter, namely the overseers are bidden to follow a path of service. But some clear distinction in titles is likely.

2. The salutation in this verse combines Greek (*charis, grace*) and Hebrew (*shalom, peace*) words in a Christian phrase. The apostle uses the conventional literary forms of his day, but there is no mistaking the rich Christian content he pours into them. Thus the customary epistolary greeting *chairein* (*cf.* Acts 15:23; 23:26) becomes the colourful *charis, grace*.

Grace is the free, spontaneous, unmerited love of God to sinful humanity, making its appearance in history and reaching its consummate expression in 'the redemption that came by Christ Jesus' (Rom. 3:24). *Peace* is the fruit of such gracious activity in the experience of sinners, and its main characteristic is reconciliation to God through Christ (*cf.* Rom. 5:1–2).[1]

II. PAUL'S THANKSGIVING AND CONFIDENCE (1:3–7)

3. Paul's further use of conventional forms of letter-writing is seen in his practice of expressing thanksgiving in the opening sentences of his epistles. Deissmann comments: 'St. Paul was therefore adhering to a beautiful secular custom when he so frequently began his letters with thanks to God.'[2] The earliest evidence of a parallel to his words *I thank my God* is in a papyrus letter, written in 168 BC by an angry wife to her husband, begging him to come home. The interest here is twofold: the mention of the prayer which the wife makes continually to the gods

[1] For reconciliation as a key to Paul's teaching and living, see R. P. Martin, *Reconciliation. A Study of Paul's Theology* (Marshall, Morgan and Scott/John Knox Press, 1981).

[2] Deissmann, *Light from the Ancient East*, p. 181. For examples of ancient letters *cf.* C. K. Barrett, *The New Testament Background: Selected Documents* (SPCK, 1956), pp. 27–29.

for her husband's safety and prosperity; and her thanksgiving for the health of her husband. Both these features reappear, in a Christian context, in Paul's letters.[1]

The preposition *epi*, introduces the occasion of the thanksgiving, '*in* all my remembrance of you' (RSV). NIV gives a looser translation 'every time I remember you', suggesting the meaning that Paul renders thanks to God whenever he thinks of his Christian friends. Another interpretation, however, is possible.[2] This would translate the words as: 'for all your remembrance of me' (so Moffatt), and see in the verse the apostle's thanksgiving to God for the prayerful remembrance which his beloved Philippians have of him in his confinement, with a side-glance at the recent money gift which they had sent him. On this view, Paul expresses his appreciation for the help, both spiritual and material, of the church, and verses 3 and 5 are linked as containing the double occasion of his thanksgiving: 'for every actual expression of your remembrance of me, and for your partnership in the gospel'. An added advantage of this interpretation of Paul's enigmatic Greek is that he expresses his thanks for the church's gift at the opening of the letter, and does not leave saying 'thank you' until a final section (4:10–20), a procedure which most readers find strange. The delayed allusion to Paul's thanks for the gift has been taken to argue that 4:10–20 is a separate 'note', but in our view this is denied by verse 3.

4. The continuation of Paul's thanksgiving is not taken up until verse 5. Hence verse 4 is parenthetic as Lightfoot and

---

[1]See P. T. O'Brien, 'Thanksgiving within the Structure of Pauline Theology' in *Pauline Studies: Essays Presented to F. F. Bruce*, edd. D. A. Hagner and M. J. Harris (Paternoster/Eerdmans, 1980), pp. 54–63.

[2]It is argued for, in great detail, by P. Schubert, *Form and Function of the Pauline Thanksgivings*, BZNTW 20 (Töpelmann, 1939), pp. 71–82. His two main points are (i) that in the other Pauline letters the construction *epi* (for) with the dative case invariably introduces the cause for which thanks are offered; and (ii) that, as in other epistles, the thanksgiving introduces 'the vital theme of the letter' or 'the epistolary situation'. The epistle was written to convey the apostle's thanks for the Philippians' gift, so here it contains an allusion to the money gift in the word *remembrance*. Therefore it cannot be Paul's remembrance of them, but must be a reference to the way they had remembered (*i.e.* supported) him by their gifts.

Gnilka show. The Philippians have remembered the apostle in his need. For this he praises God, and assures them of his supplication on their behalf, which he makes continually (*I* . . . *pray* is a present participle) and comprehensively (*for all of you* embraces the whole fellowship of believers: see the Introduction, p. 47); and he prays *with joy* in his heart. The apostle's irrepressible and constant *joy* even in the midst of his sufferings is a distinguishing feature of this epistle.

5. His thought moves on to express the ground of his thanksgiving to God: *because of your partnership in the gospel from the first day until now.* The meaning of the term *partnership in the gospel, koinōnia eis to euangelion,* has already been discussed in the Introduction (pp. 49–50). The translation 'generosity' (as in Rom. 15:26 ('contribution'); 2 Cor. 9:13)[2] seems best to cover the apostle's thought as he reflects upon the way in which the church has supported him *from the first day, i.e.* the establishment of the church through the preaching of the word, recorded in Acts 16. Their receiving the gospel message and their obedience to it are shown to be genuine by the outworking of the truth in their lives. They had abounded in the grace of unstinting generosity (see 2 Cor. 8:7), and so had proved the sincerity of their love (2 Cor. 8:8) for the Lord and his work. A sidelight in the Philippians' sacrificial support of Paul's ministry is seen in 4:3 as well as 2 Cor. 8:1–5; 9:1–5. We today might take the lesson to heart that the sign of our professed love for the gospel is the measure of sacrifice we are prepared to make in order to help its progress.

6. The beginning of the work of God in the lives of the Philippians, hinted at in the phrase 'from the first day' (v. 5), calls forth an expression of the apostle's confidence. *He who began a good work in you* is an undoubted reference to God whose redeeming grace in the gospel originated the church. Paul

---

For discussion leading to agreement with this, see P. T. O'Brien, *Introductory Thanksgivings in the Letters of Paul* (Brill, 1977), pp. 20–33, 41–46.

[2]See *IBD* 1, pp. 307, 308.

makes no personal claim to be the human founder of the church as he does at Corinth (1 Cor. 3:10), but even there he is careful to insist that the only true foundation is Christ himself (1 Cor. 3:11).

It is possible to take *a good work* as an allusion to the Philippians' participation in the apostolic ministry by their gifts: 'their co-operation with and affection for the apostle', as Lightfoot puts it. 2 Corinthians 8:6 uses almost identical verbs, 'begin, finish', for Titus' administration of the relief fund for the Jerusalem church. So, 'this "sharing in the gospel" *is* the good work referred to here' (Hawthorne).

On the other hand, Paul may be looking beyond the generosity of the Philippians to that work of grace within their lives which first gave them the impulse to contribute to his missionary labours. The *good work* would then be the action of God at the time of their conversion. This is confirmed by the way in which Paul often refers to the time when God's grace began to work in the lives of his readers (see 1 Cor. 1:4; Col. 1:5; 1 Thes. 1:5–6; Phm. 5f. and especially Gal. 3:3 where the two verbs of this verse are used).

God's redeeming and renewing work will reach its crown and climax at *the day of Christ Jesus*. This eschatological note makes Hawthorne's view that verse 6 refers exclusively to the matter of Philippian generosity in aiding the gospel unlikely. Paul is reaching out to see the wider context of their response to God's grace. He who began the work of redemption will continue to perform it until its completion when the Lord returns. The thought here stresses not only the sovereign initiative of God in salvation (*cf.* the wording of Acts 16:14, describing the first Philippian convert), but also the sovereign faithfulness of God in Christ. It reveals Paul's unshakeable confidence that the community at Philippi will be preserved in spite of its sufferings and in the face of assaults which are levelled against it (1:28; 2:15; 3:17ff.). The converse of this confidence is his appeal for unity and steadfastness (4:1). The readers are urged to stand firm (1:27) because of the mighty power of the Lord whose promise (Mt. 16:18) guarantees the preservation of the church in all its trials. 'The perseverance of the saints rests on the perseverance of God with the saints' (Motyer).

7. This confidence in God's gracious work is continued in the apostle's intimate regard for the Philippians. *It is right for me to feel this way about all of you* prefaces his assurance that he has continual thought for them, even in his imprisonment.

To feel, phronein, is a favourite expression of Paul in this letter (ten of the occurrences of the verb of the twenty-three references in all Paul's letters are here). Its range and depth of meaning can be seen by referring to 2:2 (twice), 5; 3:15 (twice), 16 (in the Received Text), 19; 4:2, 10 (twice). It means (in these verses) much more than a mental exercise or emotional reaction, and signifies rather 'sympathetic interest and concern, expressing as it does the action of the heart as well as the intellect' (Michael). It is the outworking of thought as it determines motives, and through motives the conduct of the person involved. A word like 'concern' based on the highest interests of others seems to cover most of the uses of *phronein* in our epistle.[1]

Here we find the apostle laying bare a heart of sympathy and pastoral concern for his converts who occupy a tender place in his affection. Paul was often vividly conscious of being present with his converts even when he was physically separated from them (1 Cor. 5:3–5; Col. 2:5); but this metaphor *I have you in my heart* (as in 2 Cor. 7:3; *cf.* 1 Thes. 2:17) is the most imaginative in all his writings. As Paul's Greek is cryptic, an alternative rendering has been proposed: 'because you hold me in such affection', that is, reversing the role of the Greek words *me* and *hymas*. If the understanding of verse 3 given above carries conviction, there is much to be said for this new translation. Paul is recognizing how much the Philippians took thought for him by their gifts.

The vividness of this phrase needs to be compared with *all of you share in God's grace with me;* that is, both the apostle and the Philippians share together not only in suffering and conflict but also in the grace of God. This surprising conclusion is what

[1]See further the discussion of the word under 'Thought' in A. Richardson (ed.), *A Theological Word Book of the Bible* (SCM, 1950), pp. 257, 258.

Dibelius calls 'a genuinely Pauline paradox'. The closeness of fellow-feeling is based upon a common participation (*koinōnia*) in the grace of God, and a deep sense of oneness even though the apostle and the church are separated by distance. The preposition 'with', *syn*, is a characteristic one in this letter.

Paul is a prisoner for Christ's sake and the gospel's; and he is, at the same time, suffering on behalf of the churches (Eph. 3:13; Col. 1:24; 2 Tim. 2:10). The church at Philippi is suffering with him by entering into the afflictions of his apostolate (see on 4:14–15). It is doing this by the gifts and prayers of the members, and by their unwavering devotion to Christ in the face of common adversaries (1:28–30: 'the same struggle'). Likewise the church shares in the same grace as the apostle has received , and 'grace' carries the overtone of divine strength in human weakness, as in 2 Corinthians 12:9.

Paul's being *in chains or defending and confirming the gospel* may be interpreted in two ways. It may refer to his ministry of preaching: so Motyer. In this case 'defending the gospel' means disarming prejudice and overcoming objections to the truth (for this sense see 2 Cor. 7:11), and 'confirming' means the positive declaration of the truth. Or the phrase may be taken as having to do with his imprisonment. In this case, *defending* and *confirming*, *apologia* and *bebaiōsis*, are legal terms which describe his trial before the imperial court (*cf.* 2 Tim. 4:16) or his provincial judges. The second view is taken by recent writers, such as Bruce and Hawthorne, following Moulton-Milligan who state that, on the evidence of the papyri, 'the word (*bebaiōsis*) must always be read with the technical sense in mind'. There is, then, a clear contrast in Paul's statement: 'whether I am in prison or whether I am arraigned before my judges for the gospel's sake, you all share with me in the grace of my God-given commission'.

III. AN APOSTOLIC PRAYER (1:8–11)

8. The pain of separation, intensified by his imprisonment, is expressed in the vigorous language of this verse. Paul calls God to witness that his longing[1] to be re-united with his converts is so strong that it can be described as yearning with the heart of the Lord himself (see Moffatt). *With the affection of Christ Jesus* is an elegant paraphrase for the Greek, literally 'in the entrails of Christ Jesus'. In ancient thought the viscera were regarded as the seat of emotional life (of God, Is. 63:15, as well as of man, Je. 4:19).

The compassionate regard of Jesus Christ on which Paul patterns his apostolic affection is seen in his love for his church. But many commentators see a more 'mystical' meaning in the words: for example, 'his pulse beats with the pulse of Christ; his heart throbs with the heart of Christ' (Lightfoot), as though Christ were expressing his love through the personality of his servant.

9. Such heartfelt desire to see the Christians at Philippi cannot be immediately fulfilled in view of the apostle's circumstances; and the only outlet of his feelings is in the form of a prayer, which ranks as one of the outstanding prayers of the apostle for his churches. Almost every word must be carefully weighed if the greatness and range of the petition are to yield their richness.

It is a prayer that *love* for fellow-believers may develop in the qualities of *knowledge* and *depth of insight*. The first word generally conveys the idea of a mental grasp of spiritual truth, but the biblical sense of knowing God in an intimacy made possible through his self-disclosure and received by faith is the main thought here.[2] A better *knowledge* of God and his ways will promote greater harmony within the fellowship, and give the Philippians a clearer understanding of their mutual relationships as fellow-believers. *Aisthēsis*, translated in NIV as *depth of insight*, can be understood also as 'perception', 'discrimination', or even 'tact'; it is the employment of the faculty which makes a

---

[1] The word is *epipotheō*: 'I yearn', 'desire ardently' used by Paul especially of his longing to see his Christian friends; *cf.* Rom. 1:11; 1 Thes. 3:6; 2 Tim. 1:4.

[2] *'Epignōsis'* – the word here – 'has become almost a technical term for the decisive knowledge of God which is implied in conversion to the Christian faith', R. Bultmann, *TDNT* 1, p. 707.

person able to make a moral decision. (*Cf.* the cognate word in Heb. 5:14, 'moral faculties'.) It is used in the LXX to translate 'wisdom' and 'knowledge' (especially in Proverbs *e.g.* 1:4, 7, 22; 3:20; 5:2), but is found only once in the New Testament.

These two Christian qualities were necessary in a community where a tendency to disunity and fault-finding was present (see on 4:1ff.), and needed to be put right.[1] So Paul makes this his earnest prayer before proceeding to admonition and correction. Christians, it seems, are slow to learn this valuable lesson: the most effective way to influence another is to pray for that person, and if a word of rebuke or correction has to be spoken let it be prayed over first, and then spoken in love.

10. A twofold result of the acquiring of these virtues is that they would be able (a) to *discern what is best*; and (b), on the level of Christian character and demeanour, to become *pure and blameless* in preparation for the day when God will judge the secrets of all by Jesus Christ (Rom. 2:16).

The verb *dokimazō, discern*, means 'to put to the test', and then, as a result of such examination, 'to accept as tested, to approve'. It is often used to denote the testing of coins. Those coins which are 'approved' are genuine currency. But a wider usage (*e.g.* examination of cattle, in Lk. 14:19) is also found. The object of the verb in this context may be rendered 'the things which differ' or 'the things which excel' (*cf.* GNB, and NEB and marg.). The meaning here, as in Romans 2:18 where the exact turn of phrase, which is derived from current popular philosophy, is repeated, seems to be 'the things which really matter' (*cf.* Moffatt's 'a sense of what is vital').

The fulfilment of the apostle's prayer will be that his friends will have the ability to discern, and then to practise in their Christian living, the really important issues in their corporate life as a believing Christian community. Such things would certainly include a closer harmony and the cultivation of a

---

[1] R. Jewett, 'Conflicting Movements in the Early Church as Reflected in Philippians', *NovT*, 12, 1970, pp. 362–390, summarized in R. P. Martin, *Philippians* (NCB, 1976=1980), pp. 29–34, has some interesting comment on these two words as Paul's answer to ethical problems at Philippi.

brotherly spirit, replacing bickering and dissension. The modern reader will be reminded of Augustine's dictum that the only thing which really unites people is a common desire for the same ends. As far as the Philippians were concerned, the virtues on which they were unitedly to set their hearts are listed in 4:8–9. Again, we may suspect some moral confusion in the Philippian church is at the heart of Paul's admonition. Hence he gives a call to 'choose what is best' (GNB), to discern 'the best among the good' (Bengel), which is far harder to do than preferring good to evil courses of action.

Their calling is to be *pure*.[1] This translates *eilikrineis*, a word which may possibly be derived from *heilē*, 'sunlight', which would continue the thought of testing, *i.e.* tested by the exacting standards of clear sunlight and shown to be unmixed, pure, genuine. Moffatt translates 'transparent', while GNB offers 'free from all impurity'. It is also to be *blameless*, which is almost an equivalent of the first word, unless its meaning is transitive, 'not causing stumbling' to another person. This alternative is a thoroughly Pauline expression (see 1 Cor. 10:32; and *cf.* Rom. 14:20–21), but is less preferable here (Bruce).

11. A further aspiration of the apostle for his readers is that their lives might be *filled with the fruit of righteousness*. It is clear that this is part of his prayer for their present experience and influence, rather than a looking forward to their future state at the day of Christ, as Moule takes it. The fruit (in the singular: so NIV [but not RSV] following the best MSS and in line with other references; Gal. 5:22; Eph. 5:9; *cf.* 1:22) of righteousness is either the possession of Christ's righteousness received by faith (3:9), *i.e.* fruit which consists in being right with God (so Houlden), or the evidence of such right relationship in the display of those ethical characteristics which are described in Galatians 5:22. But both views are complementary. The following clause *that comes through Jesus Christ* would lend support to the first interpretation in the light of Paul's doctrine of justification by faith in Christ. But the Old Testament background (Prov. 11:30; Am. 6:12; *cf.*

[1] See Barclay, *New Testament Words*, pp. 32, 33.

Jas. 3:12) suggests the latter, meaning 'conduct that is pleasing to God' (Wilson). At *the day of Christ* and its searching test of a person's character the real issue will be, Is that person found trusting in that divinely-provided righteousness, and practising the kind of life-style that please God? 'Salvation is the grace-filled life that bears the fruit of righteousness' (Getty). But this is equally a challenge for present self-examination. Are we now ready to demonstrate a 'faith expressing itself through love' (Gal. 5:6)? The affirmative answer is an added incentive to give *glory and praise* to God for such a marvellous provision made for the unrighteous sinner by God in the gift and work of his Son and power of his Spirit to produce such a harvest (Gal. 5:22–23).[1]

IV. PAUL'S GREAT AMBITION AND JOY (1:12–26)

It is best to take these verses together as forming one long section which is dominated by the thought of 1:18. In spite of the hostility of his enemies outside the church and the evil designs of his detractors within, the apostle is greatly encouraged by one overriding fact: Christ is being proclaimed. Indeed his very confinement, so far from curtailing the ministry of the word, has led to an extension of the gospel; and even the rivalry and misdirected zeal of his fellow-Christians in the place of his captivity cannot obscure the all-important fact that the message of Christ is being preached. Both his imprisonment with its uncertain issue, and his enemies whose presence has isolated him from sympathetic Christian fellowship (2:20–21) – circumstances which would have cause a lesser individual great frustration and despair – only increase his joy that the higher interests of the gospel are being served.

[1]For a helpful study of these verses and Paul's teaching on prayer, see G. P. Wiles, *Paul's Intercessory Prayers* SNTSMS 24 (Cambridge University Press, 1974), pp. 205–215.

A. UNEXPECTED RESULTS OF HIS IMPRISONMENT (1:12–14)

12. The information given in these verses reads like a reply to an enquiry about Paul's conditions in prison. *Now I want you to know* suggests that the Philippians may have either written or sent a message by Epaphroditus (2:25) to express their concern about his safety and welfare. Paul replies by using a standard expression – called today a 'disclosure formula' – to relate his circumstances. He tells them that the outcome of recent events, *what has happened to me* (lit. 'my affairs', as in Eph. 6:21; Col. 4:7), has *served to advance the gospel*. The meaning of this phrase, *prokopēn tou euangeliou*, is advancement in spite of obstructions and dangers which would block the path of the traveller. The chief obstacle to the fulfilment of Paul's ministry was, at this time, his enforced confinement in the praetorium (1:13). But the unexpected thing is that although his activity has been restricted in this way, the actual imprisonment has resulted in a powerful witness for Christ in the scene of his captivity, and a consequent triumph of the gospel in the pagan world (*cf.* 2 Tim. 2:9).

13. The way in which the gospel was made known was by means of his *chains for Christ*, *i.e.* the fact that he was a prisoner because of his adherence to Christ, and not because he was a political or civil wrongdoer. *For Christ* (lit. 'in Christ') may also be taken to mean that it was Paul's example of the way in which he bore his suffering *in Christ*, *i.e.* as a Christian in union with his Lord, that gave point and power to his witness.

The Greek term *praitōrion*, *palace guard* (NIV marg. *palace*), has been taken in a number of ways. The word denotes the residence of the governor of a province in the other New Testament references (Pilate's residence, as Roman procurator, in Jerusalem; Herod's palace in Caesarea). It is also used of the emperor's palace on the Palatine Hill in Rome, which is the meaning of this verse according to the traditional view; but the correctness of this identification is unlikely in view of Lightfoot's discussion of the term.[1] In this context it is more probable that

---

[1] The full note in Lightfoot, pp. 99–104 may be consulted.

Paul has in mind the progress of the gospel among persons rather than in places. *Praitōrion* can also be used of the praetorian guards, and *everyone else* seems to fix the identification as referring to Roman soldiers, wherever they were based.

The RSV rendering 'throughout the whole praetorian guard' follows Lightfoot who believed this guard to be at Rome. But the word can be used to refer to the seat of a provincial government outside Rome which was the centre of political or judicial authority in a particular province or, with a personal reference, to detachments of the praetorian guard which were posted for duty in such provincial centres.[1] We may suppose, then, that the praetorian guard would come into touch with their prisoner in the course of their supervisory duties, and *everyone else* or 'all the rest' (RSV) describes the wider circle, of both pagans and Christians, who came to hear of Paul's imprisonment and the reason for it.

14. A second consequence of his captivity was a salutary effect upon the apostle's fellow-believers. These *brothers* (the following words *in the Lord* are better construed with the words *have been encouraged*, not as in NIV) were so encouraged and stimulated by the fortitude of Paul the prisoner that they had begun to give a bolder testimony to *the word* of God than hitherto. The full phrase 'the word of God' (NIV, RSV) is strongly attested, but the KJV now supported by P^{46} and adopted by Nestle-Aland text (see Hawthorne) may preserve the primitive technical formula for Christian preaching. The boldness and fearlessness of the Christian family in the scene of his captivity is a further cause of joy to the imprisoned apostle.

Additional Note on 1:13

The evidence seems to show that if Paul was writing from Rome the reference must be, not to the emperor's palace or his judicial court, but to the praetorian guard; but if the text refers to the high judicial authority before which Paul has been arraigned

[1] See Additional Note on this word found below.

and is to be tried, then the place of writing must be in the provinces (*e.g.* Corinth, Ephesus, Caesarea). Those who champion the Ephesian origin of the letter (see the Introduction, pp. 28–36) point to the inscriptional evidence of the presence of such senatorial guard (taking *praetorium* to be equivalent to *praetorianus*) in the provinces,[1] although the value of this evidence has been challenged.[2]

The choice lies between the traditional view that Paul is speaking of the praetorian guard at Rome or, on the earlier dating of the epistle, of the senatorial guard stationed at either the provincial capital of proconsular Asia, Ephesus or the Syrian capital Caesarea-by-the-sea.[3] According to the second view, there is a supporting inscription to attest their presence at Ephesus; and as they would be fewer in number in Ephesus and Caesarea than at Rome, Paul's reference to *the whole* of the guard could be taken strictly literally.

This point which tells in favour of an Ephesian imprisonment also militates against the traditional Roman view. The imperial bodyguard at Rome numbered 9,000 *praetoriani*, and it is hard (though not impossible) to imagine that the case of one prisoner was known to them all.

For this matter of Paul's relations with imperial authorities, see further on 4:22. The whole matter of Paul's place of imprisonment is a balance of probabilities, and no decisive evidence for the origin of the epistle can be gained from this verse.

B. MOTIVES – SINCERE AND MIXED (1:15–18)

15–17. This paragraph has given rise to diverse interpretation. The important question is to settle, if possible, the identity of the group within the church at the place of Paul's imprisonment who were preaching *Christ out of envy and rivalry* (verse 15). Some commentators want to detach these verses

[1]See Dibelius, pp. 55.
[2]By Reicke, 'Caesarea, Rome and Captivity Letters' in *Apostolic History and the Gospel*, pp. 277–286 and Bruce, *BJRL*, 63, 1980–1981, pp. 263, 264.
[3]So Hawthorne, and Robinson, *Redating*, pp. 60, 77–79.

from the apostle's immediate situation, and take them as a general reflection with no particular reference to what has gone before. But this is very unlikely in spite of the lack of logical connection with the preceding verses. NIV smoothes the transition by adding that *it is true that*.

Another view is as follows. Michael, following Moffatt's translation, takes the verses as an aside which qualifies the apostle's earlier mention of the missionary activity of certain 'brethren' (v. 14). There are 'many' (NIV *most*) who are engaged in this laudable work, says Paul, but they are not all governed by the same motives; and he proceeds to distinguish between motives of *envy and rivalry* on the one hand, and of *good will*, on the other. Bruce sees no distinction in the term *most* in verse 14. Yet the idiom does seem to imply a distinction.

Who were these men who preached Christ *out of envy and rivalry . . . out of selfish ambition, not sincerely . . . from false motives* (vv. 15, 17, 18)? If we accept the view that such men formed a group within the larger company of the 'many' already referred to (in v. 14), then Paul is making a deliberate contrast. There are 'many' who are speaking the word with revived zeal but of these some are ill-intentioned in their activity. It follows, then, that they cannot be pagans using the name of Christ in blasphemy (*cf.* Acts 19:13), nor can they be heretics who are taking advantage of Paul's confinement to inculcate false teaching. They must be Christians who bore no love for the apostle personally, who were anxious to see him remain in prison, and who intended to make that imprisonment as galling and irksome as possible.

Their *envy and rivalry* were directed against him personally. Their preaching of Christ was set against a background of *selfish ambition, i.e.* squabbling in the interests of their party;[1] and their calculated aim was *to stir up trouble* (*thlipsis*, lit. 'friction', a vivid image of the painful rubbing of iron chains on a prisoner's hands and legs) *while I am in chains, i.e.* to irritate him as he lay helpless in prison and unable to defend himself. Such preaching was a hollow pretext (Gk. *prophasis*, NIV *from false motives*),

[1] See Barclay, *New Testament Words*, pp. 39–41.

devoid of reality.

But all these evil designs are in vain as far as their effect upon the apostle is concerned. 'Christ is being proclaimed' (v. 18, Moffatt) and that is the all-sufficient cause of his indomitable rejoicing. He therefore glories in his tribulations (*cf.* Rom. 5:3).

Other interpretations of the paragraph have been offered. Kennedy remarks that it is inconceivable that those in whom the apostle had confidence (v. 14) should be later described as raising up affliction for him in his imprisonment. He proposes to detach the *some* of verse 15a from the previous reference to the 'many' (v. 14), and to assume that the apostle has changed his point of view. Thus verse 15 begins a new section with no backward glance at verse 14. But, it may be urged, what about the *others* of verse 15b? Surely we are to think of these believers who preached Christ out of *good will* as being included in the general revival of evangelistic activity of verse 14?

Others have suggested that the preaching with wrong motives was not directed against Paul as an individual. The description, it is claimed, fits some misguided Christians who were making capital out of Paul's imprisonment either by preaching against the Jews who were (on this view) responsible for his detention at Ephesus (so Synge), or by deliberately courting the hostility of the civil authorities.[1] In the first view, they would then be guilty of preaching Christ out of 'partisanship' by using the weapon of preaching (*e.g.* severe denunciation of and invective against the Jews) as a counter-attack and a reprisal for what the Jews had done to Paul.

---

[1] T. Hawthorn, *ExpT*, 62, 1950–51, pp. 316 f. Manson, *Studies in the Gospels and Epistles*, pp. 161 ff. locates the scene of this contentious preaching in Corinth where he also believes the *praetorium* of 1:13 to be situated. He regards 1 Corinthians 1–4 as providing the best commentary on these verses 15–18. The different groups referred to will then tally with the splinter-groups of the Corinthian church. See further in the Introduction, p. 21.

For another reading of verses 15–17, *cf.* O. Cullmann, *Peter. Disciple, Apostle, Martyr* (ET, SCM, 1962, pp. 105 f.). He places Philippians in the Roman captivity, and notes the correspondence between the terms *envy* and *rivalry*, used in these verses and 1 Clement, which was written to the church at Rome and describes the animosity of the local Christians there against the apostles.

But the verbal agreement is not as exact as Cullmann states. The key term in 1 Clement, *zēlos*, is absent from Philippians 1 (*cf.* 1 Cor. 3:3, RV; Jas. 3:16). See the criticism of Michaelis, *Einleitung*, p. 206.

According to the second interpretation, the preachers were stirring up agitation by a message aimed at subverting Roman rule. In this way they were provoking martyrdom, inspired by the belief that suffering must be endured before the endtime which they sought to hasten. The apostle, however, condemns both endeavours as wrong and indicates that they only result in 'arousing friction (to themselves) by my bonds', *i.e.* because of my imprisonment.

A more recent understanding of the cryptic references to Christians who (a) preach Christ (v. 18) yet (b) emphasize an aspect of the Christian message that Paul cannot accept is as follows. They are motivated by envy and animosity towards him because he is a suffering apostle and so in their view he has discredited the Christian message. They have a rival missionary strategy that excels in power and glories in success, in a way parallel with other religious teachers in the ancient world.[1]

The other group of preachers were exercising their ministry out of motives *of good will* (v. 15) and *love* (v. 16), and in the awareness that the apostle was *put here for the defence of the gospel*. This defence (*apologia*: see 1:7) is an allusion to his legal trial. It may be that we should give emphasis to the words *of the gospel*, *i.e.* his friends whose work he praises know that his imprisonment is on the grounds of his devotion to Christ and his cause, and not because of any political entanglements with the civil powers.

Put here, keimai, is a military term, emphasizing the point that in prison he is enduring hardness as a good soldier of Jesus Christ (*cf.* 2 Tim. 2:3–4), and as much 'on duty' as the guards posted to watch over him are on duty in the service of Rome.

18. *But what does it matter?* is an apt translation of *ti gar*, lit. 'what then?' Paul sums up his reaction to the situation created by this conflict of loyalties. As he assesses the division within the Christian community which surrounds him, he is gladdened by one all-important fact: *whether from false motives or true, Christ is preached*.

---

[1]See Jewett, 'Conflicting Movements', pp. 362–390.

This statement has to do exclusively with the motives of the rival groups within the church, not with the content of their preaching. However much the apostle deplores the intention of those who are preaching Christ for their own ends, with mixed motives and intending to annoy or malign him, he does not condemn the substance of their message, which after all is *Christ*. The author of 2 Corinthians 11:4; Galatians 1:6–9 could never have countenanced erroneous doctrine or let slip an opportunity to combat false teaching, especially in the light of 3:2ff.

Therefore the opposing group cannot have been Judaizers or 'false apostles' whom he so trenchantly condemns at Galatia and Corinth.[1] Their Christian standing is plain, whatever their motives and principles may be. This is the overriding consideration, and the ground of his joy. Attempts (*e.g.* in Bruce) to see in verse 18 a mellowing of attitude to rival preachers differing from the Pauline spirit in Galatians and Corinthians do not convince, and fail to see a difference in the substance of what is offered as the Christian gospel.

C. PAUL'S DILEMMA, AND CONFIDENCE, IN LIFE AND DEATH (1:19–26)

19. Adding a second reason (*Yes, and I will continue to rejoice*, v. 18b) for his buoyant spirit, he is confident that he can count upon two kinds of aid at this time, human (*your prayers*) and divine (*the help given by the Spirit of Jesus Christ*). Nothing is more impressive of Paul's large humanity than his constant appeal for the prayers of his converts (see Rom. 15:30; 2 Cor. 1:11; Col. 4:3; 1 Thes. 5:25). He shows, too, his dependence upon the Spirit

[1]Lightfoot describes the factious group as Judaizers, but makes a distinction between the Judaizers of Galatia and those who, in these verses, represent an inadequate form of Christianity. Would Paul, however, have written so complacently if the truth of the gospel had been at stake? Perhaps they were Christians who were the personal enemies of Paul and who sought to provoke him to jealousy by their success in preaching or because they found his personality too forceful (Getty). If this is so, they had forgotten the apostle's teaching on love, *e.g.* in 1 Corinthians 13:4–7, 'love ... does not envy ... is not easily angered, it keeps no record of wrongs'.

who dwelt so richly in Jesus Christ (cf. Acts 16:7). *Help* translates *epichorēgia*, meaning assistance which undergirds and strengthens the object, as in Ephesians 4:16: a ligament which acts as a support. The exact nature of the help which he asks for cannot be settled until the first part of the verse has been clarified. *What has happened* is evidently a backward look at the apostle's witness to the gospel in verse 12. Then he looks forward confidently to his *deliverance* which can either be his personal final salvation (cf. Rom. 5:9 for the future tense of salvation) or to his ultimate vindication in court. But we should be careful to note that this salvation cannot be the same as his release from imprisonment in view of the next verse where he envisages the possibility of death, a consideration which Hawthorne argues does not exist.

Michael argues persuasively for the second meaning, quoting Job 13:16: 'this might turn out for my deliverance'. In the LXX the wording is identical with Paul's wording; it can hardly be doubted that the apostle is quoting the Old Testament. He is confident that whether he is acquitted or not his stand for Christ will be vindicated; and this was the expectation of Job: 'I know I will be vindicated' (13:18).

There is a third option. We may press the evidence of the Old Testament quotation even further assuming that Paul is identifying with Job's plight. Then the issue is one of being shown to be 'in the right'; for Job it was a desire to prove his integrity, for Paul he wants to have his apostolic standing vindicated against his detractors who despised him as a suffering apostle. He therefore calls on help, both divine and human, to answer his critics.

In this case the aid he knows he can count upon is the strengthening of his personal life by that Spirit whom the Lord promised to his disciples in the day of their arraignment before tribunals and magistrates (Mt. 10:20; Mk. 13:11; Lk. 12:11, 12, so Collange). He asks for the church's prayer to the same end.

20. As a consequence of this spiritual reinforcement in the testing experience of his situation he hopes that *in no way* will he *be ashamed*, especially when he is called to stand before the

77

judges' seat. Or, it may be, his role as a suffering apostle would cause his friends embarrassment (Jewett). On the contrary his 'expectation and . . . hope, (RSV) is that *with sufficient courage* (*parrēsia*, *i.e.* forthrightness in public speaking)[1] . . . *Christ will be exalted*, whether the outcome is release or martyrdom.

Apokaradokia, which is also found in Romans 8:19, is a picturesque word, possibly Paul's own coinage, which RSV translates 'eager expectation' and NIV renders as a verb *I eagerly expect*. It denotes a state of keen anticipation of the future, the craning of the neck to catch a glimpse of what lies ahead, 'the concentrated intense hope which ignores other interests (*apo*), and strains forward as with outstretched head (*kara, dokein*)' as Kennedy well describes it. So confidently does the apostle await the verdict of his trial, preoccupied not with his fate but rather with the desire that whatever happens may result in the glory of his Master. 'Perish all things, so that Christ be magnified!' was the memorable watchword of Lord Shaftesbury, re-echoing the apostle's conviction; and there is no purer desire than this, that the whole of our life and Christian service may enhance the glory and esteem of the one who alone is worthy.

In my body would confirm the view that the apostle had his destiny in mind, although some writers take the phrase to refer to his entire person which was ever at the Lord's disposal (*cf.* Rom. 14:8; 1 Cor. 6:20) in life and death. These great alternatives are set in stark contrast. If Paul is released, Christ will be magnified by a continuance of his apostolic ministry (*cf.* v. 24); if the verdict goes against him, it will still be true that Christ is to be glorified in his martyrdom by his faithful witness unto death. The alternatives, so tremendous to us, are seen by the apostle as leading to the same end: the glory of the Lord, *i.e.* Christ's glory or honour will be served (Getty).

21. The preceding verse helps to elucidate this famous Pauline affirmation which is, with verses 22–23, somewhat obscure, although the general sense is clear and the spiritual truth outstandingly impressive. Both Gnilka and Hawthorne demon-

---

[1] See W. C. van Unnik, *BJRL*, 44, 1961–62, pp. 466–488.

strate how Paul's thought proceeds from the premise of verse
20 in a series of deductions and conclusions. Yet it is not
strictly a logical progression. Scott rightly observes that 'his
language at this point is broken and obscure, reflecting the
perturbation of his mind as he turns from one alternative to
another and cannot arrive at a decision'. But we must add that
the perturbation is caused only by the claims of the alternatives, and not by the uncertainty of his future which he knows
to be entirely and securely in God's hands.

The verse may be interpreted in a number of ways which
are listed by Bonnard. The best sense is, 'For me to live is to
glorify Christ; that is why, if I die and thereby glorify him,
that will be a gain for me, a thing which I desire as it will bring
to a close my whole life of service for him.' The *gain*, then, is
not only the apostle's own receiving of his heavenly reward in
the presence of his Master (v. 23), but the promotion of the
gospel in the witness which his fearless martyrdom for Christ
will produce. That Paul has his martyrdom in mind here is
shown by the form of the words *to die* which is the aorist
infinitive, *to apothanein*. This form denotes the act of dying,
not the process (*cf.* 1 Cor. 15:31; 2 Cor. 5:14), nor the state, of
death (Moule).

Too often the apostle's words have been narrowly
interpreted as an individual and pietistical hope as in verse 23
(*cf.* 2 Cor. 5:8, 'to be . . . at home with the Lord'). Death, for
the Christian, will usher him into the immediate presence of
his Lord who fulfils his promise to every soul who dies safely
because he dies believing: 'today you will be with me in
paradise' (Lk. 23:43). But in the context of this section we
must emphasize equally the thought that death is *gain*
because, as Barth puts it, it is a gain for the proclamation of
the gospel; and Christ is magnified by the apostle's death as
by his life (v. 20) because in both he is dedicated to the service
of the Lord. *To me* is placed first for emphasis. Paul's only
reason for existence is that he may spend his life in that glad
service; and death for that cause will be the crowning service.
Wesley has captured Paul's thought here and at 2:17
admirably in the closing verse of his consecration hymn:

79

> Ready for all Thy perfect will,
> My acts of faith and love repeat,
> Till death Thy endless mercies seal,
> And make the sacrifice complete.

22–23. The agitation of Paul's mind is clearly to be seen in the broken syntax of his writing. Verse 22 reads literally as follows: 'But if to live in the flesh this (is) to me fruit of work, and what I shall choose I do not make known.' That is, I dare not reveal my preference. *To go on living in the body* (lit. 'flesh') must mean here the earthly life of the apostle, as distinct from the meaning 'to live in sin', as in, *e.g.* Romans 7:5, 18. It provides the assumption on which he bases his future hopes. He assumes – for the sake of expressing his intention – that he will survive the ordeal of the trial, and be released, although in other places he is not so optimistic. What follows? A continued life means a continued ministry, a further extension of his missionary labours and a greater opportunity to prove that Christ is his life. This is *fruitful labour, ergon,* which is a frequent term for his missionary activity. (See Rom. 15:18; 2 Cor. 10:11; Phil. 2:30; *cf.* Acts 15:38 and Phil. 1:6 for the same word for God's work through his instrumentality.) The choice is between a continuance of his work, on the assumption of a favourable verdict at court, and the sealing of his testimony with his blood, which he leaves unexpressed. When the alternative is presented to his mind he confesses: 'I cannot tell' what I would choose. Hawthorne wants to excise all human choice and sees only Paul's submission to God's will. But this is a denial of Paul's plain words.

If we make allowance for the broken sequence of the words, caused by the writer's intense feeling, there is no need to suppose that the verse has been tampered with by the interpolation of a later scribe. Michael would restore the original by removing the words from *if I am to go on living,* and would make the last words of the verse read on from verse 21: 'To me to live is Christ, and to die is gain: and which to choose I cannot tell.' This, however, just cuts the Gordian knot of difficulty, and deleting awkward words is the negation of constructive exegesis. There is little warrant for it here. We do not expect meticulous and lucid prose from a man when he is confronted with the solemn issues of life and death.

The dilemma which faces him is like the pressure of opposite forces, which keep him in a state of indecision. He is 'hemmed in on both sides' (Lightfoot's translation), and prevented by the equal strength of the opposing forces from inclining one way or the other. *I am torn between the two, synechomai*, carries the idea of external control (*cf.* Lk. 12:50; 2 Cor. 5:14). But if it were left to his own natural inclination the option would be clear: he would choose to die and to be *with Christ. Epithymia, desire*, is usually used in the New Testament in the bad sense, *i.e.* evil desire, lust. Its use here is different. The reason for this strong desire is his confidence that death provides the entrance gate to the immediate presence of Christ. *To depart* is a euphemism for death; it is a military term for striking camp (2 Macc. 9:1) and a nautical expression for releasing a vessel from its moorings. (*Cf.* 2 Tim. 4:6 for the cognate noun.)[1]

To be with Christ translates *syn Christō einai*. The preposition 'nearly always means the fellowship of the faithful with Christ after their death or after His coming'.[2] And the last phrase is vital, since Paul is able to state clearly – if paradoxically – both the expectation of Christ's presence known at death and a future hope of resurrection (3:20–21). With the pledge of being at home with the Lord after the parousia the present verse is a limpid statement of Paul's reunion with his Lord whose company he has known so vividly by faith as a pilgrim on earth. Nevertheless, although Paul lives here and now in intimate union and communion with his Lord as a 'man in Christ' (2 Cor. 12:2), the expectation he here expresses is of an even closer intimacy and deeper fullness beyond death than he has previously known.[3] This future 'being-with-Christ' is *better by far*, lit. 'much rather better', a triple comparative meaning 'by far the best'.

Any idea of an unconscious state following death or of a purgatorial discipline in the next world is denied by the sheer

---

[1] See G. M. Lee on verses 22–23, *NovT*, 12 (1970), p. 361.

[2] Deissmann, *Light from the Ancient East*, p. 303, n. 1.

[3] See the full discussion by George, *Communion with God*, pp. 150–155, and M. J. Harris, *Raised Immortal* (Marshall, Morgan and Scott, 1983).

simplicity of Paul's expectation. Many things about the future beyond the grave are veiled from us; but what has been revealed is all we need to know. 'So we will be with the Lord forever' (1 Thes. 4:17; *cf.* 1 Thes. 5:10), a promise permitting us to face the challenge of Mary Ann Getty's remark, 'The moment of death is the ultimate test of faith.'

24. But this personal desire 'to be with Christ' in glory must be subordinated to his pastoral responsibility to the Philippians. Into the scales of his choice there goes not only his natural 'desire to depart' but, on the other side, the down-to-earth needs of his fellow-believers; and this is the heavier weight. It is *more necessary for* them that he should remain, if God so decree, and more in harmony with the divine will for the church, the care of which was always a powerful factor in his thinking and planning (2 Cor. 11:28).

25. The opening tone of this verse expresses what has appeared to many scholars as a new confidence. The atmosphere of verses 20, 23 was heavy with the thought of imminent martyrdom and it seemed that death was just around the corner, so that Michael can write, 'Paul . . . in his inmost heart anticipated for himself no other fate than death.' It is possible to say that the present verse simply continues the supposition that Paul is considering his own desires and merely expressing 'a personal conviction based on his sense of the Philippians' need of him', as the same commentator puts it.

This may be so; but substantial reasons have been suggested for a new confidence of release. Was it a prophetic illumination that God gave him that the issue would be favourable? Or favourable news that came to him about his judges' decision? Or a meditation which led to a firm conviction that all would be well? Here we are left to guesswork because there is no sure evidence on which to build. It may be wrong to exaggerate this confident feeling, especially in view of 2:17 where the apostle returns to the distinct possibility that he will not escape from his fate of martyrdom.

At all events, the mood of this verse, whether there were firm grounds for optimism or not, is one of assured expectation. His confidence is that he will *continue* (the Greek adds 'and remain', a doubling of synonymous verbs for emphasis) with his beloved friends at Philippi. He envisages a return to them, and a resumption of his ministry in their midst. *Progress, prokopē*, is the same word as in 1:12, but here it applies to the progress of the believer's spiritual life based on a deepening of *joy* and an enlargement of *faith*. 'The only progress Paul would be concerned to forward would be the progress of their faith' is Michael's wise comment; and the apostle sets himself forward as an example of one who was seeking constantly to make such progress (see 3:12–14). We may include the thought that their *faith* or possibly their grasp of the faith they professed would be confirmed by the answering of prayer in his safe return. His 'coming to them again' (v. 26, RSV), if it were God's good pleasure, would certainly promote their *joy*.

26. NIV's rendering *your joy in Christ Jesus will overflow* is more of a paraphrase and places the emphasis on Paul's hope of a return visit to Philippi rather than on the way this visit will affect his readers. See RSV which keeps the word order and describes what the Philippians would feel if Paul were restored again to the church. *Kauchēma* is really 'boasting,' or 'exultation'. The Philippians would have ample cause for gratitude to God in the release of their human founder and his renewed presence, *parousia*, with them. The glory would be given to God whose mercy would be recalled, but Paul's triumphant experience (*on account of me*) would be the occasion of this outburst of exultation, possibly as they heard from his lips the record of the Lord's gracious dealings with him in his confinement. The setting of this important verse has been spotlighted by R. Jewett.[1] As Paul is restored to the Philippians his return in the providence of God will demonstrate his genuine apostleship even though he is called to suffer. This release is not a cause of shame (1:20) but confirms the credibility of his apostolic status which the Philippians may well have doubted. Here Paul calls them to 'boast' – a

[1] Jewett, 'Conflicting Movements', p. 387.

83

strong word – in his weakness, just as he does (2 Cor. 12:1–10). His 'coming' like a royal visit (*parousia*) will vindicate Paul in their eyes.[1]

V. EXHORTATIONS TO THE COMMUNITY
(1:27 – 2:18)

It is necessary to see this entire section as a unity with no break at the artificially made chapter division after 1:30. The apostle's thought runs on to 2:18, and includes the celebrated section of 2:5–11, which is a hymn of the humiliation and exaltation of the Lord of glory stretching back to the past eternity of his pre-incarnate oneness with the Father, and reaching forward to his ultimate triumph and acknowledgment by every creature. But, even if the hymn is an independent composition and inserted in the section as a separately composed piece of Christian liturgy, it is well integrated into the letter, and firmly set within the framework of a pastoral exhortation. See the Additional Note on 2:5–11 (pp. 110–114).

'What Paul expects from the church' is one summary of 1:27 – 2:18. This expectation is occasioned by some wrong-headed thinking and understanding of the Christian life. Recent studies of the problems at Philippi have traced the presence of an idea which Paul regarded as alien to his gospel. At its heart was the misguided eschatology that believed the Christian community to be already raised with Christ to a heavenly life begun here and now. The practical outworking was that Christians believed their life to be exempt from hardship and suffering with a consequent disdain of Paul's sufferings as an apostle. The other side of this claim was that the Christian vocation and commitment to lowliness and altruistic regard was forgotten; hence ugly symptoms of selfish egotism and pride needed to be diagnosed and treated. Paul's response meets these needs, as we shall see, and in particular, he focuses on the nature of

[1]For Paul's movements, including possible visits to Philippi, see Ogg, *The Chronology of the Life of Paul,/The Odyssey of Paul.*

Christian living as 'in Christ' whose story of salvation is told in a dramatic way (2:6–11).

A. EXHORTATION TO UNITY AND COURAGE IN THE FACE OF ALIEN INFLUENCES (1:27–30)

27. The future hopes of the apostle and the prospect of a reunion with the Philippians now give way to a stirring call and exhortation. He turns to consider the inner life of the Christian community which is set forth against the background of some fierce pressure on the Philippian community.

Paul sets the standard he desired to see in the opening admonition, *Whatever happens* (Gk. *monon*, lit. 'only'. Paul raises a warning finger: so Barth), *conduct yourselves in a manner worthy of the gospel of Christ*. This sentence very skilfully joins together the inner state of the church, which needed a reformation and amendment in the practical matters of true love and mutual concern, and its present danger which is that it will succumb to the pressure of false teachers whose presence we may see in verse 28. To be sure, the 'opponents' may be the pagan world and its persecuting powers, as most commentators hold. But if Paul's warning in chapter 3 is a continuation of the same call to alertness, then the Philippians are being warned against those whose version of the Christian message and life is at odds with Paul's gospel (Hawthorne).

Monon is placed first and is emphatic. The meaning is, then, 'above all, at all costs' as in Galatians 3:2. The joyful spirit of the apostle which nothing can daunt would, however, be saddened if the Philippians failed to show themselves worthy of the message of Christ. They must not disappoint him as he lies in prison by lowering the standard of their church life, and refusing to live up to their citizenship to which the gospel has called them. With consummate tact the apostle presents the standard and encourages his readers to reach it before addressing himself to the obvious faults and failings mentioned in later verses.

Worthy of the gospel recalls similar phrases in other Pauline letters (*e.g.* Rom. 16:2; Eph. 4:1; Col. 1:10;) in which he insists upon the very highest standard as the pattern of the believers' behaviour. Christians have a high calling to fulfil. They have received some amazing privileges as children of God, members of the body of Christ and heirs of eternal glory. But let them not only be appreciative of all the good that has come through the gospel of Christ; let them also recall that 'rank imposes obligation' (*noblesse oblige*) and 'from the one who has been entrusted with much, much more will be asked' (Lk. 12:48). His 'manner of life' as 'a new creation' in Christ Jesus (2 Cor. 5:17) should reflect his gratitude and be the visible proof of the grace which the gospel has brought to his heart (*cf.* 1 Jn. 3:18).

The life of the Christian in the company of the church is likened to the citizenship (*politeia*) which the citizens of Rome enjoyed in the ancient world. So the verb *politeuesthe* here is literally rendered by some commentators 'behave as citizens'. 'Let your life as citizens' is the best translation because it brings out the precise flavour of the word more than NIV; and Paul, in view of 3:20, evidently had the local background of this group of 'citizenship' words in mind. In Acts 23:1 the verb does not have this nuance, but is the colourless 'I have lived' (*cf.* RSV).

Philippi, as a Roman colony, was intensely proud of its privileges. See the Introduction, pp. 17–18, for the benefits which being a Roman colony conferred. These privileges were gratefully accepted as a source of satisfaction and civic pride, as Claudian in a later century expressed it:

> Rome! Rome alone has found the spell to charm
> The tribes that fell beneath her conquering arm,
> Has given one name to the whole human race,
> And clasped and sheltered them in fond embrace.[1]

The populace of Philippi had voiced such sentiments of pride in Acts 16:21, and, no doubt, the native Christians shared in this feeling about their status as citizens of 'the leading city' (Acts 16:12) of the region. The apostle does not condemn this (*cf.* Rom. 13:1–7), but uses it to enforce the lesson of their double allegiance. The Philippians are Roman *cives*, with privileges to

---

[1]Quoted by T. R. Glover, *Paul of Tarsus* (SCM, ⁴1938), pp. 123, 124.

enjoy – and responsibilities to fulfil! They must equally remember that as citizens of a heavenly realm (see 3:20; Eph. 2:19) they are called not only to accept the benefit of this gospel but also to model their lives according to the pattern laid down therein. This reference to their obligation stems directly from the meaning of *politeuma* as defined by Dibelius. It signifies, he says, 'a colony of foreigners whose organization reflects in miniature the *politeia* of the homeland' (see also on 3:20). They are to be true to their membership of that new city 'which has Christ for its king, the Gospel for its law, and the Christian as its citizen' (Benoit). At a later time, Polycarp reminds the same church to be worthy citizens of his community (*Phil.* 5:2).

The appeal for a worthy life is reinforced by the reminder that Paul's visit is in the balance. *Whether I come and see you or only hear about you in my absence* is a message of caution that they should not wait for his return but put a reformation of their church life into effect immediately, so that what he hears about them at a distance may be an encouragement to him. Indeed, on the strength of 1:7, we may believe that Paul's intimacy with the Philippians was so close and his regard for them so tender (4:1) that he had only to mention this appeal to ensure that it would be effective. Yet there is an apprehensive note here, which may suggest that all is not well at Philippi. False ideas are in the air, and Paul hopes the believers will be alert to detect their danger.

What he longs to be assured of is their steadfastness, *that you stand firm*, and unity, *in one spirit*, displaying lion-hearted courage, *contending . . . without being frightened in any way by those who oppose you*. The summons to an unyielding maintenance of their testimony is repeated in 4:1, 'stand firm in the Lord'. From the later verse's addition, 'in the Lord', it is clearly possible to take *one spirit, heni pneumati*, as a reference to the Holy Spirit (so Moule, Bonnard and Motyer) rather than a call addressed to the Philippians' own disposition, as in Moffatt's 'a common spirit' or Lohmeyer's paraphrase, 'inner compactness'. The Holy Spirit strengthens the human spirit under trial, so the two interpretations are not mutually exclusive. 1 Corinthians 12:13 and Ephesians 2:18, however, seem to show that the person of the Holy Spirit is the primary meaning here. He whose office it is to unify believers in the body of Christ is the 'sphere' in which the Philippians are to maintain a courageous witness even as Paul himself leans heavily upon the same strengthening grace in his prison experience (1:19).

On the other hand, if, as it may be thought, the rivalry in the church was over the matter of superior spiritual gifts, the *ta pneumatika* of 1 Corinthians 12:1, the call might be a corrective reminder that it is the 'one Spirit' who is the author of these gifts of his grace, *ta charismata* (1 Cor. 12:4), and that he gives them in his sovereign wisdom to whomsoever he pleases (1 Cor. 12:11). Therefore there is no room for jealousy because they are *gifts* (cf. 1 Cor. 4:7) and also because the divine Spirit retains the right to give and to withhold.[1]

The Philippians' attitude to these pressures must be based on an internal harmony. Courage in their commitment to Paul's gospel and unity as the badge of their church life are combined in the words *contending as one man, synathlountes*. The simple verb, without the prefix *syn*, 'with', 'together', is found in 2 Timothy 2:5, and carries the association of contest in war and in the arena where the gladiatorial struggle was one of life and death. The preposition indicates the necessary unanimity of true community life within the church. Moffatt renders excellently, 'fighting side by side'. This imagery would remind the Philippian readers of the phalanx, consisting of a body of trained spearmen who fought in closed ranks. This was a tactical device used by Philip of Macedon and his son Alexander the Great (Wilson).

Furthermore their unity is to be 'with one mind' (RSV), *mia psychē, i.e.* presenting a united front, and not weakened by internal disaffections and rivalries. NIV renders *as one man*, but *psychē* refers rather to the believer's inward disposition (Motyer). The divided state of the church was a cause of sorrow to the apostle, and a danger to the church itself in face of the constant threat of the adversaries arriving on the scene. The

---

[1]See R. P. Martin, *The Spirit and the Congregation. Studies in 1 Corinthians 12–15* (Paternoster/Eerdmans, 1984) for the link between wrong eschatology and the proud profession of charismatic gifts.

Christians' fight, then, is on a double front. Negatively, it is against their foes (v. 28) in refusing to be intimidated and cowed by them. Positively, they are striving together *for the faith of the gospel*.

What object are they striving to maintain? *The faith* seems to be the objective content of their testimony, the 'grand deposit' of Christian truth committed to the church (1 Tim. 6:20; 2 Tim. 1:14; Jude 3) to proclaim to the world. 'Faith of our fathers! Holy faith' has been the rallying call of God's people in every age, and never more so than in days of persecution and doctrinal laxity. 'There is no agreement (possible) unless there is agreement as to what constitutes the gospel' (Motyer). The enmity of surrounding paganism and the more insidious inroad of false teaching (3:18ff.) will set the Philippians on their guard, and inspire them to maintain the faith against the latter, and to resist boldly the former, 'not caring two straws for your enemies' (v. 28, Phillips).

28. As they bravely bear their witness the Philippians are counselled against being in any way *frightened* by their opponents. Paul expresses the negative very strongly. *Frightened, ptyromenoi*, is a vivid term, unique in the Greek Bible and denoting the uncontrollable stampede of startled horses. What brought about this onslaught of fear, which they are to resist and overcome, was the power of those who distorted Paul's gospel, *antikeimenōn*. This descriptive word has a wide range of application, embracing the enemies of Jesus in the gospel records (*e.g.* Lk. 13:17), the opponents of the apostle at Ephesus (1 Cor. 16:9) as well as the anti-christ of 2 Thessalonians 2:4, and Satan, the adversary of God and man (1 Tim. 5:14–15). The application of the term in this verse has raised several possibilities. It may suggest the influence of alien teachers within the Philippian church or the presence of Roman authorities who later began to play the role of persecutors. *Those who oppose you* could also be a veiled reference to mob violence, the hatred of the Philippian populace (2:15) against the infant company of believers, whose purity of life and consciousness of high calling in Christ Jesus (3:14) were a constant challenge and rebuke to their pagan neighbours. The Jewish element of the local population may have aroused this hostility, as at Thessalonica (Acts 17:5); but it appears that the Jews were not numerous at Philippi. There is no mention of a synagogue there in Acts 16, and Acts 16:20 indicates a certain antipathy to Jews as such. A small group of them, however, may have been vociferous in arousing local sympathies against the Christians who were drawn mainly from the heathen world (see the Introduction, pp. 19–20).

If we take the evidence of 1:30 at all seriously, Paul makes a comparison between the conflicts in which he was engaged on his first visit to Philippi and at the time of writing, on the one hand, and the disturbances at Philippi on the other. It seems to have been local opposition which was the responsible cause in each instance; and, if this is so, it would tell against the Roman dating of the letter. At Rome (Acts 28: 30–31), there was nothing comparable with the persecution of Acts 16 (*cf.* 1 Thes. 2:2), and it is necessary to suppose an appreciable worsening of the apostle's state in his Roman confinement to make it correspond with the suffering of a 'struggle' (*agōn*). On the other hand, there is evidence of mob violence at Ephesus (see the Introduction pp. 28–30) in which case the opponents of both Paul (*cf.* 1 Cor. 16:9) and the Philippians will be of the same type.

This evidence appears even more cogent if Paul's allusion is to his detractors who opposed both his teaching and his purpose as an apostle whose life was marked by weakness and suffering (the background to 2 Cor.: see 2 Cor. 11:13 – 12:13). Then, Paul's struggle is to preserve the integrity of his picture of the Christian life and his role as the apostle. Verse 29 is the key to this interpretation. And Philippians and 2 Corinthians share a common setting, namely when Paul was at Ephesus, about AD 55.

The enmity levelled against believers, and their endurance under such trial, are signs of two facts: the 'perdition' (as in 3:19, 'destruction') of their opponents, and the 'salvation' of the believers themselves. And God is the responsible agent of the whole situation, as the words *and that by God* indicate. 'It is God who sends the persecutions they must undergo, the solid resistance with which they must confront them, and the assurance of salvation which follows', comments Benoit, citing 2 Thessalonians 1:4–7 as illustration.

The fact that the Philippians are being attacked has a double edge, though Hawthorne[1] offers a novel exegesis which makes the Philippians' loyalty to the gospel a proof drawn by the opponents that this adherence leads to ruin. On the more usual reading the suffering seals the doom of the persecutors as the enemies of the gospel, and it confirms the eternal salvation of the faithful who endure to the end. See Mark 13:13 and Romans 13:11 for this meaning of 'salvation' as the ultimate state of persevering believers but including the thought of God's preserving care extended to them in their trial. The Philippian Christians are to stand fast in the apostolic faith in spite of their affliction; but it is only the Lord who enables them to stand in their evil day (Eph. 6:13; *cf.* Rom. 14:4 for this interplay of human responsibility and divine grace in another context).

On one view, the persecution of the church by ungodly powers is, in every age, a great trial to faith. Why does the omnipotent and all-merciful God allow his people to be exposed to the tyranny and violence of evil forces in the world? Possibly the young church at Philippi was so beset by these doubts and fears as to deny either the power or the goodness of God in their distressing situation. Paul, therefore, would help them to a clearer understanding of his purpose by supplying, after the fashion of the Old Testament prophets (*e.g.* Isaiah, Habakkuk, Jeremiah), a theodicy of current events by interpreting their persecution in the light of divine principles. These principles include the faithfulness of God in preserving his church in every age so that 'the gates of hell' do not prevail against it, and the judgment which he executes upon all who set themselves in opposition to his truth.

The other reading of these verses sees the opponents as those who enticed the Philippians into believing that there was no place for suffering in Christian experience. Believers were already 'raised in Christ' and 'perfect' (3:12–15), and so free from all trial in this life. Paul must offer a retort to this false idea. He

[1]See his essay, Hawthorne, *ExpT*, 95, 1983, pp. 80 f.

does so by showing how suffering is integral to Christian witness, and this is a sign of fidelity – and of God's faithfulness in preserving (the meaning of *saved*) the church in time of trial. This trial is the temptation to abandon Paul's teaching and denigrate him because he is a suffering apostle.

29. The sovereign control and purpose of God, even in the experience of violent antagonism to the gospel, is further insisted upon in the words: *For it has been granted to you* (*i.e.* by God; this passive form is to be understood as a common feature of Hebrew thought) *on behalf of Christ . . . also to suffer for him.* Therefore, there is no accident in their suffering, nor is it a mark of divine punishment as though God were angry with them. On the contrary, it is a sign of his favour, 'seals of adoption to the children of God', as Calvin says. Not only does suffering for Christ's sake fulfil the purpose of God for his people in the world (Acts 14:22; 1 Thes. 3:3; 2 Tim. 3:12), it comes as a gift of his grace. *It has been granted, echaristhē,* is derived from *charis,* 'grace', 'favour'. This reminder is an encouragement and consolation to the afflicted people of God in all ages. To suffer *on behalf of Christ,* which can mean the same as 'for the faith of the gospel' (v. 27), is actually a privilege given by God; and with the affliction of his followers Christ himself identified, as Paul would vividly recall from his Damascus road encounter. His former animosity was directed against the Jerusalem Christians, but Christ was sharing their suffering (Acts 9:4-5: 'I am Jesus, whom you are persecuting'; *cf.* Is. 63:9). So the Philippians were called, not only to the privilege of believing in him – the ability to believe and the act of faith being itself a gift of God – but equally to endure privation and pain *for him,* as did the apostle himself (2 Cor. 1:5; 12:10). The Corinthian controversy provides a window of access through which we can see what Paul's conflict (2 Cor. 7:5) was and how he needed to justify his gospel of the suffering Lord (2 Cor. 13:4) and his apostle (2 Cor. 4:7-12).

30. Paul makes it clear that there was a correspondence between the Philippians' suffering and that which he was called upon to bear. *The same struggle* (*agōn*) was endured by both apostle and church. The emphasis is undoubtedly upon the word *same*, reminding the readers by way of encouragement that they shared, in far away Philippi, not only in the same fight for the faith and against possibly the same kind of resistance to encroachment (see v. 28), but also in the same grace by which they could together be more than conquerors through him that loved them (1:7).

They had heard of his present imprisonment and, no doubt, were wondering how he was faring in captivity. They were puzzled over his role as their leader who wore chains (1:13, 17). His letter will set their minds at rest on that score, at least. His chains are evidence 'for Christ' (1:13), as his faithful servant under the banner of the cross.[1] He is overcoming his depression in a spirit of confidence, even if the issue is uncertain and the *struggle* against his foes is fierce, with fightings without and fears within; and they can be encouraged to do likewise in their struggle. *Agōn* is used elsewhere to describe his physical hardships at Philippi (1 Thes. 2:2; 'strong opposition') and the 'conflict' of Colossians 2:1. But there is an equally relevant background in 2 Corinthians 1:8–10.

B. EXHORTATION TO HARMONY AND HUMILITY IN THE FACE OF FACTIOUSNESS (2:1–4)

1. The word *therefore* (original Gk.) looks back to 1:27, and is a bridge between the apostle's call for the unity of the church in the face of threats and a continuation of that summons for such concord and harmonious community relations as will gladden his heart.

There is a fourfold ground to his appeal that all divisiveness and enmity within the church should be resolved, and in his mind there was nothing more certain than the realities to which he appeals. Hence *if* is better rendered 'since'; or, if the NIV wording is retained, it needs to be qualified by such a phrase as 'as is indeed the case'. Paul has no doubt that the matters on

[1]See E. Stauffer, *TDNT*, 1, p. 139.

which he will ground his entreaty are definite realities in the experience of the Christians whom he is addressing.

Each of the four 'grounds of appeal' presents its own problem to the interpreter. *Encouragement, paraklēsis,* can be translated 'exhortation' as in 1 Corinthians 14:3 (AV), and is so taken by most commentators. If we adopt this meaning, the part-phrase 'in Christ', which follows on directly, will be an apostolic authorization which Paul adds on to his admonition here and later in the letter (4:7). So Hawthorne who renders, 'If . . . I have given you encouragement in Christ'. He appeals to them as one having authority from his Lord. Or it may be that Paul has in mind some specific exhortation of our Lord's, such as an early tradition of the teaching of John 17 where he prays that his people 'may be one' (17:22). NIV takes it to be the reason for the encouragement which is then given a specific content: 'encouragement from being united with Christ'. But this is interpretation rather than translation.

Another spiritual reality which should bind the Philippians together as members of the household of faith is *love*. It is by the constraint (*paramythion;* NIV *comfort*) of love, *i.e.* Paul's love for them or their fraternal regard for one another, that they should settle their differences. The *love* spoken of may equally be Christ's love for his church (so Barth, quoting 2 Cor. 5:14; *cf.* Eph. 5:25), a preferred interpretation since the phrase evidently looks back to 'in Christ'.

Any fellowship (koinōnia) with the Spirit is a well-known *crux*, which is discussed in the Introduction (see pp. 50–51). It is generally agreed that the meaning must be 'fellowship with, participation in the Spirit' (so NIV, GNB) rather than 'fellowship wrought by the Spirit' (but Bruce seeks to join the two meanings). The gift of the Holy Spirit and the believer's conscious experience of his indwelling and activity are the starting-points of the apostle's appeal. He takes it as a commonly accepted truth which can be verified by personal experience that the believers know this *koinōnia* with the Holy Spirit in all his gracious ministry to their hearts and lives. See the appeal of Acts 19:2 and Galatians 3:2–5. Their common sharing in the Spirit ought to be a decisive factor in their corporate life as 'one body in Christ'

(Rom. 12:5). This doctrine should sound the death-knell to all factiousness and party spirit, for as there is 'one Spirit' by whom they were all baptized into one body (1 Cor. 12:13) and one Spirit in whom they all share by virtue of that incorporation into Christ and in their access to the Father (Eph. 2:18), so there can be only 'one body' (Eph. 4:4) in which all are members. Such membership demands that they keep the unity of the Spirit in the bond of peace (Eph. 4:3). This is the basic theological foundation of all Christian unity. The emphasis is on 'life in the Spirit' as a precondition of the unity the Spirit gives (against Hawthorne).

Tenderness and compassion is a phrase to be taken together as hendiadys: so Dibelius who translates 'affectionate sympathy'. Colossians 3:12 supports this. The Greek *splanchna* is the viscera as the seat of the emotional state, usually expressed by Christian authors in terms of tender feelings (so Lightfoot), see on 1:8; *compassion* translates *oiktirmoi* which signifies the outward expression of deep feeling in passionate yearning and action. The apostle is grounding his call on the power of sympathy, whether it is the Lord's sympathy for his church in its obvious need as a divided community, or the pastoral interest of Paul as expressed earlier in 1:8. There is no need to make a hard and fast distinction between the two in the light of what he says in the earlier verse.

No thoughtful reader can be unmoved by the complexity and seriousness of Paul's stirring appeal. Instead of a word of superficial advice that they should sink their differences and live together in peace, he would turn their minds to the high themes of these opening words of the section. He would persuade and influence them by the lofty motives of the Lord's own will for his church that it should be one in him because he is one with the Father; of the constraining power of love which finds its origin in God's love for humankind (1 Jn. 4:7–12, 19); of the Philippians' joint-participation in one Spirit, the Lord and giver of life; and of the qualities of kindness and tender sympathy which a Christian ought to feel for his fellow-believers. To divided Christendom, and to every local church in which division and party strife are spoiling the fellowship and marring the witness, these profound truths are addressed in every age.

2. Paul's joy will be complete if only these words of appeal are responded to and adjustments made in the church's domestic life as God's family. That there were serious problems at Philippi can hardly be doubted, though Bruce tends to minimize them. He regards the disagreement of 4:2 as an isolated case. But the evidence of a deep malaise is more widespread (see Introduction pp. 40–41). The fourfold appeal is to lead to a fourfold result if the desired ends are to be achieved. These are that the church should be *like-minded* (RSV, 'of one mind'; *cf.* 3:15), *having the same love* (which answers to the 'love' of verse 1), *being one in spirit* (lit. 'together in spirit' as in 1:27, although the word may mean 'wholeheartedly'), *and [one] purpose* (which repeats the verb *phronein* used earlier in the list). This piling up of expressions which all bear upon church unity is intentional. The Philippians are left in no doubt as to the apostle's desire for them that they should share a common outlook, 'as you are one in heart with other people so you will be of one mind with them' (Collange). Thus undesirable features will be removed and unity and amity will prevail.

3. The ethical terms used here expose the spiritual malaise at the heart of the church, and point to the all-sufficient remedy. *Selfish ambition*, *eritheia* (RV, 'faction') is the same word as in 1:17 where it is used to describe the inimical intention of Paul's enemies. Of the Philippians it is used of party squabbles and petty conceits. We might translate it 'quarrelsomeness', although that does not quite convey the hint of self-seeking which the word contains. Such a display which Galatians 5:19–21 brands as an 'act of the sinful nature' sadly disfigured the inner life of the church. But there is worse to come in the diagnosis. If *selfish ambition* is the symptom of the malady the root cause may be seen in *vain conceit*, lit. 'empty glory', which is equally reprobated in Galatians 5:26. 'Factiousness and vanity,' comments Michael – 'these were the evils that menaced the Christian community at Philippi. The former is often the bane of active, vigorous Churches.' The empty conceit and unworthy ambition which are indicated by the second term are usually the cause of the trouble. This expressive word *kenodoxia* looks on to the claim to perfection refuted in 3:12–15. Paul anticipates his objection to this claim (to have 'glory' now) by remarking that only at the parousia (3:20) will 'bodies of glory' be possible. Thus to claim what could only be possible at a future state was a form of vain glory (Collange).

The antidote to these evil tendencies lies in the cultivation and practice of a characteristic Pauline virtue, *humility, tapeinophrosynē*, which he uses of himself in Acts 20:19. It is, as Bonnard expresses it, a humility before God which leads to a humility in our relations with other people. The best commentary on these two allied meanings is 1 Peter 5:5–6: we are to clothe ourselves 'with humility towards one another' as we humble ourselves 'under God's mighty hand'. Unless our *humility* begins in a recognition of our creaturely dependence upon God and our true condition in his sight, it will only show itself to the world as humbug and the false self-depreciation of the Uriah Heep variety. True biblical humility was frowned upon in the ancient world as despicable because it was misunderstood as abject cringing before one's fellow-men. L. H. Marshall, who writes a full study of the word, comments: 'It was apparently through the teaching of Jesus that humility came to be regarded as a virtue.'[1] An exception to this statement may be adduced from the life and example of the Qumran covenanters. They cherished humility as a virtue and made it the basis of the unity they sought in their monastery life. Paul's thought runs parallel but is unique in its appeal to Jesus. So he is laying the ground for his citation in 2:8 where the verb 'he humbled himself', *etapeinōsen heauton*, echoes the noun here.

To have this attitude to God and to one's fellows is also to be aware of one's own foibles and failings; and this is the mainspring of the counsel which follows: honour one another above yourselves (see Rom. 12:10). Paul not only gives the advice expressed in the word *tapeinophrosynē* which he himself might have coined; he practises what he preaches. See 4:12, where 'to

---

[1] L. H. Marshall, *The Challenge of New Testament Ethics* (Macmillan, 1946), p. 93.

be abased' (RSV) is really 'to be humbled', *tapeinousthai*.

4. Does the apostle admonish his readers to consider the 'interests' of other people (as in Moffatt), or is he concerned to fix attention upon the gifts, the spiritual endowments which are to be seen in other people's lives? If the answer is settled by the meaning of *look* it may be the second alternative, because *skopein* is used by Paul with the sense, 'regard as your aim' (Lightfoot). The good points and qualities in one's fellow-Christians are to be watched for, recognized when they appear and emulated in our lives. This gives a good sense, and is preferable to Moffatt's 'each with an eye to the interests of others as well as to his own'. Moreover, it prepares for the reference to the incarnate Lord in verses 5–11, and is conceivably Paul's gentle correcting of the self-centred preoccupation of a perfectionist group at Philippi (see 3:12–15). Their egocentric demeanour and haughty attitude had destroyed the *koinōnia* (fellowship) spirit in the church.

We are, then, not to be so preoccupied with our own concerns and the cultivation of our own spiritual life that we miss the noble traits to be seen in others. In the customary understanding of verses 5–11, we are to set our aim upon the figure of him who said 'I have set you an example' (Jn. 13:15) and in whose footsteps we are to place our feet (1 Pet. 2:21). Another approach to the verses that follow is possible, and is recommended in the light of the tenor of the stately hymn Paul quotes. The ethical call is not 'follow in Jesus' steps', but accept a way of life that befits those who live under the rule of the exalted Lord. Paul's citation of the hymn is to remind the Philippians how they came to be 'in Christ' and by reciting the 'story of salvation' to call them to conformity to his 'way', both incarnate and exalted. Paul is not placing Jesus' earthly life before their eyes as a model for imitation and certainly not as one model among many. Much more importantly, Paul is recalling the significance of Christ as saving event (Getty).

This consideration of the excellencies in another's character, and especially the picture of one who was condescending in his coming to earth and who now has the 'right to rule' will check any tendency to 'vainglory', *i.e.* pride in our own moral attainments, on the one hand, and merciless fault-finding with someone else's failings, on the other hand.

C. THE 'WAY' OF CHRIST (2:5–11)

5. The Philippians are here faced with the greatest possible incentive to unity and humility in the picture of the Lord himself whose *attitude* is described in the noble verses which follow. While this is true, the meaning of the present exhortation is more exactly: 'Let this mind be among you, as also in Christ Jesus', which is the literal translation. There is no verb in the second part of the sentence, and some recent commentators supply, not the verb 'to be' (though C. F. D. Moule has offered reasons to retain this verb: see p. 103), but the same verb as in the first part. (See Hawthorne for a variant.) Grayston gives the admirable rendering: 'Think this way among yourselves, which also you think in Christ Jesus, *i.e.* as members of His church', commenting 'This attitude of mind (described in verses 1–4) they are to have in their personal relations, because it is the only attitude proper to those who are "in Christ".' This interpretation gives to 'in Christ Jesus' the regular Pauline meaning of 'in union with Christ', which is often tantamount to 'in the fellowship of his people'.

In fact, verse 5 holds the key to all that follows, and since the Greek is cryptic with no verb in the second half, it becomes an important exegetical issue to know what verb to supply.[1]

Thus 'among you' (*en hymin*) does not imply the inculcation of personal virtue based on a moral example, but means 'in your church fellowship', so sorely harassed by strife and plagued by arrogance. Paul, by the citation of the hymn to Christ in verses 6–11, would show, in an unforgettable and convincing manner, that the community created by the incarnate and enthroned Lord must share his spirit, and be controlled by the pattern of

---

[1]The options are set out in Martin, *Philippians* (NCB, 1976=1980), pp. 91–93, with preference given to Grayston's suggestion referred to above. See also Craddock for helpful comment.

self-effacement and humility which his incarnation and cross supremely display. One of the topics to do with this passage that has occasioned much discussion is whether the basis of Paul's ethical appeal is some kind of 'imitation of Christ' or a grounding of Paul's call to unity and humility in a way of life befitting those 'in Christ', whose mind-set is determined by the events of salvation celebrated in the hymn of verses 6–11. All are agreed that the appeal of the hymn serves a hortatory purpose; the question is, What is the nature of this exhortation? Is it a call to follow in Jesus' steps by taking the pattern of these verses as example, or to respond to life 'in Christ' as those who have entered the community of salvation by obedience to the incarnate, obedient and now exalted Lord? The second option is followed in this commentary, as Paul's purpose is thus understood. No one has seen the issue more clearly than James Denney.[1] An extended quotation makes the point: 'When Paul thinks of (the glory of Christ) he does not look back, he looks up . . . men [and women] were saved, not by dwelling on the wonderful words and deeds of One who had lived some time ago, and reviving these in their imagination, but by receiving the almighty, emancipating, quickening Spirit of One who lived and reigned for evermore. . . . And so it must always be, if Christianity is to be a living religion.' This intention of the apostle leads on directly to the Christological section.

6. The following notes try to give the meaning of the words in the text. See the Additional Note (pp. 110–114) for a consideration of the form, style and authorship of the verses.

Being in very nature God looks back to our Lord's pre-temporal existence as the second person of the trinity. The verbal form translated *being, hyparchōn*, need not necessarily mean this, but it seems clear that this sense is the only satisfactory one in the context. RV margin translates 'being originally', and this must refer to the pre-incarnate state to which Paul elsewhere makes reference (see Rom. 8:3; 1 Cor. 10:4; 2 Cor. 8:9; Gal. 4:4). 'The form of God' (NIV margin) may be taken in two ways. The older

---

[1] *Second Corinthians*, Expositor's Bible (Hodder & Stoughton, 1894), pp. 140–141.

commentators (*e.g.* Gifford, Lightfoot, followed by Hawthorne) interpret the term in its philosophical sense as here
meaning the essential attributes of God 'in a sense substan-
tially the same which it bears in Greek philosophy'.[1] A newer
view suggests that there is a connection between 'form',
morphē, and the term 'glory', *doxa*.[2] When this fact is applied
to the apostle's teaching on the person of Christ there is ample
attestation that he saw in the pre-existent and glorified Christ
both the image (*i.e.* 'form') and glory of God (2 Cor. 4:4; Col.
1:15); and these terms are rooted in the Old Testament
tradition of Adam as created in the image of God (Gn. 1:26–27;
cf. 1 Cor. 11:7) and reflecting the divine *kabōd* or splendour
(Ps. 8:5 hints at this) which he subsequently forfeited at the
fall.

Equality with God is again a phrase which has been taken in a
number of ways. The main issue is whether it is equivalent to
being in the 'form of God' (Hawthorne), or is to be regarded as
something future in the 'experience' of the pre-incarnate and
incarnate Lord and which he could have attained but refused
to do so.

Some writers regard the first possibility as correct in one of
two ways. On the one hand, it is held, following Lightfoot,
that the pre-incarnate Son already possessed equality with the
Father and resolved not to cling to it. Or, on the other view,
he had no need to grasp at divine equality because he already
possessed it as the eternal Son of God. It is questionable,
however, whether the sense of the verb can glide from its real
meaning of 'to seize', 'to snatch violently' to that of 'to hold
fast'; and the second interpretation hardly does justice to the
structure of the whole sentence as well as to the force of
'exalted to the highest place' in verse 9. Attempting a different
approach, Kennedy and those who see as a background here
the Genesis story and the temptation presented to Adam to 'be

[1]Lightfoot, p. 132; *cf.* E. Gifford, *The Incarnation* (Longmans, Green, 1911 edition), pp.
12 ff. and Hawthorne, pp. 83, 84.

[2]See the present writer's contribution in the *ExpT*, 70, 1959, pp. 183, 184, and *Carmen
Christi* (Eerdmans/Paternoster, ²1983), pp. xix–xxi, 102–120.

like God' (Gn. 3:5)[1] draw the parallel between the first and the last Adam. The former senselessly sought to grasp at equality with God, and through pride and disobedience lost the glorious image of his maker; the latter chose to tread the pathway of lowly obedience in order to be exalted by God as Lord (v. 9–10), *i.e.* to be placed on an equality which he did not have previously, because it is only by 'the suffering of death' that he is 'crowned with glory and honour' (Heb. 2:9, RSV).

Something to be grasped is one translation of the key-word *harpagmos* which may be taken actively as in AV/KJV or passively as in RSV: 'did not count equality with God a thing to be grasped'. Both versions are linguistically possible. The real difficulty is encountered in the questions: Does it mean that Christ enjoyed equality with God and surrendered it by becoming man, or that he could have grasped at equality with God by self-assertion, but declined to do so and embraced rather the will of God in the circumstances of the incarnation and the cross? Or is the hymn saying that 'Jesus reckoned God-likeness not to be snatching' (C. F. D. Moule)?

Here once more, if the key to the text lies in the intended parallel between the first Adam and the second Adam, one of the latter options is to be preferred; and this is the generally prevailing modern view which Stauffer believes has been definitely settled: 'So the old contention about *harpagmos* is over: equality with God is not a *res rapta* . . . a position which the pre-existent Christ had and gave up, but it is a *res rapienda*, a possibility of advancement which he declined.'[2] There is, however, another possibility which may be briefly stated as follows.[3] *Harpagmos* can have the meaning of 'a piece of good fortune, a lucky find'. Bonnard takes the illustration of a spring-board (*tremplin*) with the same essential thought of an opportunity which the pre-existent Christ had before him. He existed in the divine 'condition' or 'rank' as the unique image and glory of God, but refused to utilize this favoured position to exploit his

---

[1] See especially J. D. G. Dunn, *Christology in the Making* (SCM/Westminster, 1980), pp. 114–121.

[2] E. Stauffer, *New Testament Theology* (ET, SCM, 1955), p. 284, note 369.

[3] It is developed in my *Carmen Christi*, pp. xxi–xxiii, 134–164.

privileges and assert himself in opposition to his Father.

The key-word *harpagmos* is here interpreted as the holding of a privilege which opens up the future possibility of advantage if only the possessor will exploit it to his own profit. In his pre-existent state Christ already had as his possession the unique dignity of his place within the Godhead. It was a vantage-point from which he might have exploited his position and, by an assertion of his right, have seized the glory and honour of the acknowledgement of his office. At this point he made his pre-incarnate choice. He considered the appropriation of divine honour *in this way* a temptation to be resisted, and chose rather to be proclaimed as equal with God as the 'Lord' by the acceptance of his destiny as the incarnate and humiliated one.

This verse has given rise to such diverse opinion that it seems presumptuous to state baldly an interpretation and pass over in silence much that has been suggestively and plausibly written. All we can do here is to pursue one line of enquiry that seems to be the most fruitful for an understanding of these profound words.[1] The association of thought is the Old Testament, and there is an implied contrast between the two Adams. Less probably it has been proposed that the temptation and fall of Satan (see Is. 14) as interpreted by later Jewish writers is the clue to the passage (so Stauffer).

'The form of God' (RSV; NIV *being in very nature God* is more an interpretative paraphrase rather than a rendering of *en morphē theou*) takes us back to the 'status' of Christ in eternity. Attempts to deny this aspect[2] come to grief on the requirement (from v. 6b) that the element of choice necessitates a 'state' to be left – his pre-temporal glory (John 17:5) – if he is to become incarnate. Yet once we are firm at the point of Christ's pre-existing we can see how the model of the 'two Adams' could have dictated the

---

[1] A fuller presentation of the problems and solutions of these verses is attempted by the author in the Tyndale Lecture, *An Early Christian Confession: Philippians ii. 5–11 in recent interpretation* (Tyndale, 1960), and further in *Carmen Christi: Philippians 2:5–11 in recent interpretation and in the setting of early Christian worship* SNTSMS, 4 (Cambridge University Press, 1963; Eerdmans/Paternoster ²1983) and *Philippians* (NCB, 1976=1980), pp. 94–98. Of the many recent studies one deserves special mention: C. F. D. Moule, 'Further Reflexions on Philippians 2:5–11' in *Apostolic History and the Gospel*, pp. 264–276.

[2] *E.g.* in Dunn, *Christology in the Making*, pp. 114–121.

flow of the passage. Adam in Genesis 1 reflects the glory of the eternal Son of God who from all eternity was 'with God' (Jn. 1:1; 17:5) as the exact image of the ineffable and invisible God (Heb. 1:3). The 'act of robbery' was attempted as Adam, the son of God (Lk. 3:38) and made a little lower than God (Ps. 8:5, NIV marg.), asserted himself to be 'as God' (Gn. 3:5, 22), *i.e.* to be lord in his own right and independently of God his maker. But he failed in this aspiration.

The eternal Son of God, however, faced with a parallel temptation, renounced what was his by right, and could actually have become his possession by the seizure of it, *viz.* equality with God, and chose instead the way of obedient suffering as the pathway to his lordship. The circumstances of this tremendous decision are described in the verses which follow.

7. The upshot of the momentous choice of verse 6 is here recorded. As he did not clutch at equality with his Father he perforce accepted the consequences of this renunciation. *But made himself nothing*, which is, more literally, 'but emptied himself', *heauton ekenōsen* – a phrase which has given its name to the so-called 'kenosis' theory of the incarnation[1] – is best interpreted in the light of the words which immediately follow. It will then refer to the 'pre-incarnate renunciation coincident with the act of "taking the form of a servant" ',[2] and this reading of the text stands over against the original 'kenotic' idea that in becoming man he divested himself of the relative attributes of deity, *viz.* omniscience, omnipotence and omnipresence, and even suffered the extinction of his eternal self-consciousness. The present verse says nothing about such things, but rather teaches that his 'kenosis' or self-emptying was his taking the servant's form, and this involved the necessary limitation of his glory which he laid aside in order that he might be born *in human likeness*.

---

[1] See Beare's commentary for kenoticism, pp. 159–174 (E. R. Fairweather's essay). There are some acute criticisms of and comments on this theory in L. Morris, *The Lord from Heaven* (Tyndale, 1958), pp. 73, 74.

[2] V. Taylor, *The Person of Christ in New Testament Teaching* (St. Martin's/Macmillan, 1958), p. 77, and my short contribution to *IBD*, 2, pp. 848, 849.

The very nature of a servant is taken by most older exegetes as a vivid description of his humanity. He shared our human nature in all its frailty and finitude (Rom. 8:3; Heb. 2:7, 14), and entered upon his earthly life circumscribed by the restrictions imposed by that nature with the glorious exception that he was without sin. His true stature was concealed in the weakness of his mortality, and his glory was veiled in his humanity. The 'kenosis' was this act of self-abnegation in which his native glory which he had enjoyed from all eternity (Jn. 17:5, 24) was laid aside in his becoming man.

There is another possibility, however, which starts from the position that *servant*, which is, in Judaism, a title of dignity (so Lohmeyer quoted earlier on p. 57), may here refer to the servant of God *par excellence*, the Suffering Servant of Isaiah's prophecy. Admittedly the LXX translates the Hebrew *'ebed Yahweh* by *pais* and not *doulos* as in the verse here, but this is not an insuperable difficulty as both terms are used interchangeably, and Aquila reads *ho doulos* in place of the LXX *ho pais* in Isaiah 52:13.

Much has also been made of the use of Isaiah 53 in understanding verse 7. The expression of our text *heauton ekenōsen*, 'he emptied himself', is found nowhere else in Greek and is grammatically harsh, a fact which may point to an underlying Semitic original, of which our verse is a translation. Jeremias finds this original in Isaiah 53:12: 'he poured out his life unto death', declaring that 'the expression implies the surrender of life, not the *kenosis* of the incarnation'.[1] This novel exegesis, which had been recognized earlier but never taken seriously in the commentaries, removes the verse completely from the theology of the incarnation and concentrates all attention upon the cross as the price he paid in obedience to the divine will for our redemption. But there are difficulties.[2] It may well be that the hymn speaks of Jesus' acceptance of *doulos* for simpler reasons: (1) to establish the role of Jesus as one of Israel's righteous sufferers, called 'God's servants'; (2) to mark out Jesus as having no rights or privileges and so to underscore his decision to 'give

[1] J. Jeremias, *The Servant of God* (ET, SCM, 1957), p. 97.
[2] Noted in Martin, *Philippians* (NCB, 1976=1980), pp. 97, 98.

himself away' (v. 8: so Moule); and (3) to set up an antithesis with what he is given by God's grace, the rank and name of 'Lord' (v. 11).

8. The further description of *being found in appearance as a man* appears simply to repeat what has been said in the previous sentence, and those who stress the metrical and liturgical structure of the hymn (*e.g.* Dibelius) regard this merely as a piece of poetic repetition. But it does make plain that our Lord was truly man and not only that he became *like* a man (as v. 7 'being made in human likeness' might suggest). On the other hand, some scholars, especially Lohmeyer, have lessened the force of this unequivocal statement of the Lord's humanity by treating the phrase *in appearance as a man* as representing an Aramaic term, *kᵉbar 'ᵉnāsh*, meaning 'as a son of man, *i.e.* a man carrying the appearance of a divinity as in Daniel, Enoch and the Ezra Apocalypse, *i.e.* chapters 13 of 2 Esdras in the Apocrypha (*cf.* Rev. 1:13; 14:14). This title could mean, on this reading, not his humanity but his transcendental state as the heavenly man who came to earth to accomplish a saving mission for the world. The doctrine of the heavenly man has been traced elsewhere in Paul's writings (*e.g.* 1 Cor. 15:45ff.), but not convincingly. Bruce sees a parallel in verse 8 to Daniel 7:13–14 but in the sense that the one who 'looked like a human being' (GNB) is now exalted as the 'one who received from God such power and honour' that his kingdom is forever.

In the search for parallels it is better to consider the phrase as suggesting a connection between the two Adams based on the Genesis account; or, more preferable still because it prepares for what follows, to relate it to the presentation of the figure of the Servant of the Lord in Isaiah 52:14 or 53:3. *He humbled himself* refers to his entire life upon earth in its devotion to the Father and the acceptance of our human lot. But undoubtedly the climax of his life is most prominently in view, namely, his humiliation in the passion and death at Calvary. Here there is a parallel in Isaiah 53:8 where the LXX reads *en tē tapeinōsei* corresponding to *etapeinōsen heauton, he humbled himself.*

His obedience is a sure token of his deity and authority for, as

Lohmeyer says in a brilliant insight, only a divine being can accept death as *obedience*; for ordinary people it is a necessity. He alone as the obedient Son could choose death as his destiny; and he did so because of his love, a love which was directed both to his Father's redeeming purpose and equally to the world into which he came: 'I have come to do your will' (Heb. 10:7). It is this complete embracing of the will of God which gives value to his culminating obedience *to death*. But we must not be too quick to read the text as though it said explictly that obedience was rendered to God. It does not, and leaves open the question. Perhaps it says no more than that Jesus' whole life was one of submission, for this is the determining characteristic of a slave who owes all obedience to his master (Collange).

The solemn words *to death* perhaps signify more than the utter limit of his humiliation. They may contain a hint of a descent to the underworld and enslavement by the demon power of death (Lohmeyer; this idea is taken up by Käsemann, quoted on p. 113, and Beare). For this thought of the tyranny of death, see Hebrews 2:15. However strange this idea may seem to us, it lies firmly embedded in the New Testament (see Acts 2:27, 31; Rom. 10:6–8; Eph. 4:8–10 and, above all, 1 Pet. 3:19).

Death on a cross must be understood from two points of view. It would have special meaning for the Christian readers who were resident in a Roman city where revulsion against this form of capital punishment would be strong. 'This most cruel and hideous form of punishment' is the way it is described by Cicero, who expresses his feelings about crucifixion as follows: 'Far be the very name of a cross, not only from the body, but even from the thought, the eyes, the ears of Roman citizens'.[1]

It will also be remembered that the writer was a Jew (3:5) to whom death by Roman crucifixion came under the rubric of Deuteronomy 21:23 and meant that the victim was outside the pale of Israel, and that he was under a ban of excommunication from God's covenant. It was this thought which proved the stumbling-block of the cross to the Jew (1 Cor. 1:23); but, to Paul the Christian, it became the very nerve-centre of his doctrine of

[1]See the wealth of detail in M. Hengel, *Crucifixion* (ET, SCM, 1977).

the cross and reconciliation (see Rom. 5:1–11; 2 Cor. 5:21; Gal. 3:13).[1] But here the teaching of the purpose of the cross is assumed. It is the fact which is alone stated, and some scholars find in this omission evidence of the pre-Pauline authorship of the hymn. See the Additional Note, pp. 110–114. At all events, the story of Christ reaches its first climax at this point. These three stanzas (vv. 6–8) lead in one great sweep, from the highest height to the deepest depth, from the light of God to the darkness of death (Lohmeyer).

9. At this juncture in the sequence of thought the chief actor in the drama of incarnation and atonement changes. Attention has, up to this point, been focused on the self-humbling and obedience of the Son of God. Now it is God who, as it were, takes the initiative. And the name of Jesus Christ is introduced; it is absent from verses 6–8.

The obedience of Christ the Son is crowned by the act of exaltation in which the Father raises his Son from the dead and elevates him to the place of honour. The resurrection and glorification of the Lord are the Father's response to the filial obedience which led him to the cross. This pattern of exaltation following humiliation is thoroughly biblical, and especially evident in the teaching of Jesus (see Mt. 18:4; 23:12; Lk. 14:11; 18:14; *cf.* 2 Cor. 11:7; Phil. 4:12).

Therefore (giving the result of his obedient submission to death) *God exalted him to the highest place* (giving the verb an elative or superlative sense, which is probably correct) is a phrase including the resurrection which is tacitly assumed, but it is aimed primarily at expressing the truth of the ascension as in Acts 2:33 (*cf.* Acts 5:31).[2] The LXX uses the same verb, here translated *exalted*, Isaiah 52:13. Bruce sees a link with Daniel 7:13–14 as we have noted.

He who stooped so low is now lifted up to the glorious rank of equality with God, *i.e.* the enjoyment of that dignity which was

---

[1] See also Martin, *Reconciliation*.

[2] Exaltation is described pictorially as sitting at God's right hand, which denotes co-regency, *i.e.* the receiving and enjoyment of a dignity equal with God: so W. Foerster, *TDNT*, 3, p. 1088.

ever his by right but which he never clutched at as his personal possession. The elevation is, then, not in regard to his nature or inherent place within the Godhead. It is rather an ascription to him of what could only be his after the submission and sacrifice of his earthly life, and specifically relates to his lordship as king of the universe.

This honour now conferred is expressed by the bestowal of *the name*, *i.e.* a character, which he chose to assume not by right or seizure (the *harpagmos* of v. 6), but by obedient humiliation. The honour which he refused to arrogate to himself is now conferred upon him by the Father's good pleasure: *gave him* (*echarisato*) bears this sense of 'granted by the exercise of a favour' (*charis*). The human name 'Jesus' is important not least because it declares that lordly power is seen as committed to the hands of the historical person of Jesus of Nazareth, who is not some cosmic cipher or despotic ruler but a figure to whom Christians could give a name and a face. This factor controls the next assertion about his office as Lord.

In the light of verse 11, the supreme name is that of 'Lord'. The root meaning of this term (*kyrios*), used in the LXX to translate the divine name Yahweh, though with a possible Christian influence at work, denotes rulership based upon competent and authoritative power, the ability to dispose of what one possesses. In view of its special connection with the name of God in the Old Testament the giving of the name in this context declares that Jesus Christ is installed in the place which properly belongs to God himself as Lord of all creation. Of this fact there are, according to the subsequent verses, two outstanding proofs.

10–11. In his name, the name which is above every name, *every knee* must *bow*, and *every tongue confess* (*i.e.* proclaim) *that Jesus Christ is Lord*. Both aspects of this acknowledgment are based on Isaiah 45:23 in a context which proclaims the unique greatness of Israel's God. No clearer proof could be forthcoming of our Lord's pre-eminent position at the Father's right hand than the use of this Old Testament quotation in reference to him. Yet we should also trace here a claiming of a

Jewish prooftext for the oneness of God.[1] On the other hand, he occupies his exalted status *to the glory of God the Father.* His throne is no rival to his Father's (Rev. 3:21), but his lordship is based upon the sovereignty and express intention of the God whose purpose is that he might gather in one all things in Christ (Eph. 1:10; *cf.* Eph. 1:20-23) so that ultimately God might be all in all (1 Cor. 15:28).

The cosmic authority of our Lord Jesus Christ is expressed in the triadic phrase, *in heaven and on earth and under the earth.* These words are represented in the Greek by three adjectives with connecting particles. The AV/KJV and RV take the adjectives to refer to implied neuter nouns, hence 'things' (so Lightfoot). This view concludes that if the adjectives are neuter the most we can say is that the text speaks of 'the overall notion of universality of homage to God'.[2] But it is more likely that the reference is a personal one, as in the parallel thought of Ignatius (*Trallians* 9.1). It is intelligent beings in heaven, earth and the underworld (see GNB) who bend the knee in submission and whose lips make the confession which formed the earliest Christian creed, *Jesus Christ is Lord.*

Additional Note on 2:5-11

In the course of the commentary on these verses some of the main trends in the modern discussion have been mentioned. On the matters of authorship, style and background, the following supplementary points may be noticed.

In recent years the section of Paul's letter covered by these verses has been treated as a Christological hymn. The evidence for this is found in the stately and solemn ring of the words and the way in which the sentences are constructed. The words are obviously carefully chosen, with the result that, when the verses are read aloud, the stress falls in such a way as to give a rhythmical cadence to the lines. When the text is written in the

---

[1] See Martin, *Carmen Christi*, pp. xxv-xxxiii.
[2] So also W. Carr, *Angels and Principalities*, SNTSMS 42 (Cambridge University Press, 1981), pp. 86-89.

form of poetry this fact is more easily appreciated. We must also take into account the presence of extremely rare words. Lohmeyer's conclusion in his work *Kyrios Jesus*[1] is now generally accepted, that what we have here is an early Christian confession which belongs to the literature of liturgy rather than epistolary prose.

Lohmeyer, however, goes further. He maintains that the hymn was originally composed by a Christian poet whose mother tongue was Semitic and sung at the celebration of the Lord's Supper by the church in Palestine. Moreover, because of this view of its origin and the use of words which are not found again in Paul's writings, he submits that the author cannot have been the apostle himself. To support this denial of apostolic authorship it is claimed that many of the ideas which are familiar Pauline teaching are absent. The redemptive significance of the cross (the phrase, 'even death on a cross' is removed in Lohmeyer's analysis because it breaks the metrical structure of the hymn), the emphasis on the resurrection, which is not mentioned separately from the exaltation of the Lord, and the role of the church are cases in point.

Paul's debt to his Christian predecessors, those who were in Christ before him (see Rom. 16:7), is a subject which has been much to the fore in recent New Testament studies.[2] As far as the present 'hymn to Christ' is concerned, the choice is between the view that Paul inherited this early Christian confession and introduced it into the hortatory section of the letter as a sublime reinforcement to his appeal that the Philippians should accept the implications of their calling 'in Christ Jesus', or the view that Paul himself composed the passage at an earlier time and now utilized it to buttress his pastoral concern for the Philippian church. To decide between these alternatives would take us into a technical discussion.[3] We may note, however, two points which are relevant. First, if the section is a hymn set in liturgical

[1]E. Lohmeyer, *Kyrios Jesus* (Winter, 1928=1961).

[2]See A. M. Hunter's comprehensive treatment, *Paul and His Predecessors* (SCM, 1940, revised 1961).

[3]Details of this discussion, together with a bibliography, may be found in the author's *Carmen Christi*, ch. 3, updated by *Philippians* (NCB, 1976=1980), pp. 109–116.

111

style, this fact may in itself explain some of the unique features which have been detected, such as the rare vocabulary and the absence of ideas which the apostle elsewhere elaborates in detail. His choice of words and theme would be governed by the type of composition he has in mind. Secondly, we know from such a passage as 1 Corinthians 13 that Paul was capable of an exalted, poetic style. Yet we also know that he drew on tradition, especially credal formulations (1 Cor. 15:3-5), and Christological teaching (Col. 1:15-20). On balance, and with some tentativeness the data point to 2:6-11 as containing traditional teaching, a preformed hymnic tribute which Paul took over from his predecessors.

What does appear as certain is that these verses, whatever their authorship may be, are distinctive and are in the form of a quotation which Paul is making to support his appeal to the Philippians. They are, as Hunter puts it, 'like a "purple patch" stitched into the fabric of the exhortation'.

As to the form of the verses, we would expect that if they are really in the nature of a hymn it would be possible to arrange them into stanzas or strophes. And this is so, as Lohmeyer has demonstrated. He prints the text in such a way as to produce a hymn of six stanzas, each with three lines.

   I Being in the form of God,
     He considered it not a thing to be seized
     To be equal with God;

  II But emptied Himself,
     By taking the form of a slave,
     Coming in human likeness.

 III And appearing on earth as Man,
     He humbled Himself,
     Becoming obedient unto death (indeed, death on a cross).

 IV Wherefore God exalted Him,
     And bestowed on Him the name
     That is above every name;

V That in the name of Jesus
Every knee should bow,
In heaven, on earth, and under the earth,

VI And every tongue confess:
'Jesus Christ is Lord',
To the glory of God the Father.

Later discussion has suggested a modification of this arrangement, but at the cost of removing certain phrases from the text in the interest of metrical harmony. Jeremias' reconstruction emphasizes the three aspects of our Lord's existence, *viz.* his pre-existence, incarnate life and exalted status as Lord, by his arrangement into three stanzas as follows. Stanza I comprises verses 6 and 7a; stanza II, verses 7b and 8; stanza III, verses 9–11. But this requires the excision of some phrases ('in heaven and on earth and under the earth', 'to the glory of God the Father' as well as 'even death on a cross') in order to achieve the result of a perfectly balanced hymn. If that is an achievable goal and not a will-o'-the-wisp, as Hawthorne thinks, a setting down of these verses to form a series of antiphonal lines in couplets is possible.[1]

On the matter of background there is a wide variety of interpretation. Continental scholars, especially those who 'demythologize' the New Testament, see the hymn against the background of Hellenistic or gnostic notions of a 'heavenly man' who descended to earth and carried through a mission of redemption for humankind.[2] The influence of this theory on the outlook of the apostle must be seriously questioned in spite of certain formal resemblances between the myth and the terms which he uses to express his understanding of Christ.

The Old Testament, we believe, provides the most intelligible background to these verses (so Caird, Getty, Bruce, Hawthorne). The two concepts which are most likely to underlie the

---

[1]See Martin, *Carmen Christi*, pp. 36–38; an analysis accepted by Collange and others.

[2]See, for example, E. Käsemann, 'A Critical Analysis of Philippians 2:5–11', in *Journal for Theology and Church*, 5 (Harper, 1968), pp. 45–88. But this proposal is criticized by W. Pannenberg, *Jesus, God and Man* (ET, SCM, 1968), pp. 151–154.

apostle's thought are the teaching concerning Adam, and the notion of wisdom as developed from Proverbs 8 by the inter-testamental writers (Sirach 24; Wisdom of Solomon ch. 2–7). His existence in the divine form as God's image patterned on wisdom's role, and his refusal to grasp at equality with his Father find their parallel in the story of the first man and his temptation. The obedience, humiliation and exaltation of the Lord are also foreshadowed in the picture of the Suffering Servant of Isaiah 52–53. It is this fusion of ideas, under the directing Spirit of God, which gave to the early Christian community in Syria and Antioch, and, it may be, through the infant church especially in the school of Stephen,[1] to the apostle himself, this noble presentation. It is the record of the pre-existent, humiliated and glorified Lord who is ever the object of the church's worship and the destined Ruler of all created life.

D. EXHORTATION APPLIED, AND THE EXAMPLE OF PAUL (2:12–18)

12. The two main emphases of the hymn to Christ in the preceding verses were his obedience (2:8; *cf.* Heb. 5:8) and his receiving the title of Lord (v. 11; *cf.* Rom. 14:9). Both aspects of his 'way' likened to an odyssey from one eternity to another are now applied to the Philippians' situation, and *therefore* is the connecting link between the story and the application. As he obeyed, so should you! As he is now Lord, so live under his rule! But this is no stern, military-like command, untempered by love. The apostle softens the exhortation by inserting *my dear friends* as a reminder that his commands, like those of God in whose name he speaks, are not grievous (1 Jn. 5:3), but are the loving expression of his pastoral heart.

He knows that the Philippians were obedient to him as God's messenger during his stay (Acts 16). In fact, it was their obedience to the gospel (*cf.* Acts 16:15, 33) which, on its human side, first brought the church into being. Paul often reminds his readers of their initial obedience to the gospel's call and claim

---

[1] Martin, *Carmen Christi*, pp. 297–313.

(*e.g.* Rom. 6:17; 16:19) and expects a continuing obedience to his apostolic directives (*e.g.* 2 Cor. 7:15; 10:6; 2 Thes. 3:4; Phm. 21).

Now *in my absence* they are called upon to show the same spirit of submission to God's will as was expressed in his admonitions to unity and courage. The physical *presence* of Paul with the church is not possible because of his confinement, although in his optimistic moments he looks forward to reunion with the Philippians (see 1:26). In other parts of his letter he fears the worst as the outcome of his captivity and trial (see Commentary on 1:20; 2:17) and *in my absence* may hold an ominous fear that his martyrdom will prevent any further contact with them. At a distance, then, and with the future in the balance, he yearns for them (see on 1:7–8) and he confidently appeals for their obedience in the pressing matter of their church life which needed reformation.

The situation of discord and fearfulness at Philippi controls the exegesis of the present verse and the entire section. *Continue to work out your salvation* has often been wrenched out of its context and made the basis of a theological discussion which, however true and necessary in a general statement of New Testament theology, is not relevant in this section of the letter. Thus the contrast is often made between what the Philippians are to do, *work out*, and God's activity mentioned in verse 13, and applied to the outworking of personal salvation. We are to 'work out', as Müller puts it, what God in his grace has 'worked in'.

It seems clear, however, that the true exegesis must begin with a definition of *salvation*, not in personal terms, but in regard to the corporate life of the Philippian church. The readers are being encouraged to concentrate upon reforming their church life, 'working at' (Moffatt) this matter until the spiritual health of the community, diseased by strife and bad feeling, is restored. *Salvation, sōtēria*, can have this meaning as in Acts 27:34, 'your health' (NIV paraphrases: 'you need it to survive') and the verb *work out, katergazesthe*, is better rendered 'work at'. *Your own, heautōn*, can hardly be taken in a personal sense (*cf.* Müller, 'your *own* and not that of one another') since the apostle is urging the Philippians to have their eyes fixed on the interests of others (see Commentary on 2:4) and not to be preoccupied with their own concerns. The reference here must look back to 1:28, where the salvation of the Christian community as a whole is in view.

The tenor of the passage confirms this interpretation, which is forcefully stated by Michael[1] and accepted by later commentators, *e.g.* Hawthorne. After the great passage of 2:5–11 it would be singularly inappropriate to stress personal salvation; and the following verses are best understood if their reference is to the attitude of the Philippians towards one another in the fellowship of the church.

The attitude with which they are to face this task is one of humility, *with fear and trembling*, and complete reliance upon God for his strength in carrying it through (v. 13). The apostle uses the identical phrase in 2 Corinthians 7:15 and Ephesians 6:5, where again it is the attitude to men which is described. So here it denotes the spirit which should characterize the mutual relationships of the Philippians.

13. The much-needed restoration of harmonious relationships within the church, its corporate 'salvation', can only be produced in dependence upon God's power. They can only 'work out' this reformation as God *works in* them, as the connecting word *for* indicates. *In you* is taken by Michaelis and I. H. Marshall to mean 'in your hearts', and naturally the spirit of reconciliation and harmony must be born there if it is to be effectual in the community. But 'among you, in your midst' is a better rendering, as in 2:5 where the same phrase is used.

The wording here makes it clear that God is effectively at work in the Philippian church. He is described as he *who works*, *ho energōn*, a verb which denotes effective working (see note on 3:21 where the noun *energeia* is used). His action is in the matter of 'willing' and 'working'; the latter verb *to energein* repeats the description of God given earlier. He produces both the will to

<hr />

[1]See his commentary *ad loc.*; and more fully, *Expositor*, 9th series, 12, 1924, pp. 439–450. See too I. H. Marshall, *Kept by the Power of God* (Epworth, 1969), pp. 113, 114 for a critique. But verse 13, 'in you', taken to mean 'in your hearts', can hardly support his objection.

amend the condition of his people and brings about the accomplishment of this state of 'goodwill', *eudokia*, in their midst.

This interpretation takes *to his good purpose* to mean not so much God's goodwill expressed towards the Philippians 'in fulfilment of His benevolent purpose' (Lightfoot), but rather the pattern of goodwill which his gracious activity promotes in the fellowship as he inspires the *will* and energizes the achievement of amicable relationships. *Eudokia* may be regarded as an equivalent of the Old Testament term *ratsōn*, in which case it refers to the will of God who shows his good pleasure in choosing and blessing his people (as in Lk. 2:14, according to the most recent interpretation, based on the evidence of the Dead Sea Scrolls). But that it can equally mean human goodwill is shown by 1:15 (*cf.* Rom. 10:1; 2 Thes. 1:11, where it may be rendered 'every resolve of goodness'). So Michael, Collange, and Hawthorne.

The choice, then, is between taking *eudokia* to refer to God's intention that his people should be united in a fellowship of love; or to mean, as Michael puts it, that 'goodwill should characterize the Christian community'. In both cases it is only God's action that can secure the desired result.

14. A 'social' interpretation of these verses is confirmed by the indictment of *complaining or arguing*, the sins which stained the shield of the people of God in the Old Testament (*cf.* Ex. 16:7; Nu. 11:1). Not only did they complain about Moses; more seriously, they rebelled against God himself (see Ex. 16:8). The parallel, however, is not an exact one because it is more likely that the *complaining or arguing* of the Philippians was directed against one another than against God (against Beare, Caird). There is no suggestion of a break in the thought of the previous verses, and the apostle continues his warning against grumbling and wrangling in the church fellowship. *Arguing, dialogismoi*, may be taken in the manward, legal sense of 'dissensions', 'litigation', as the evidence of the papyri shows (see Moulton-Milligan, who suggest 'outward disputing and discussion'). It is conceivable that the plague of settling quarrels at pagan law-courts had broken out at Philippi as at Corinth (see

1 Cor. 6:1–11). If so, this would represent an advanced stage of the petty rivalry and desire for 'vain conceit' (2:3) which was the root evil at the heart of the church. The other symptom is described as *complaining, gongysmoi,* an evil-sounding word, used also of a plague spot in the Corinthian community (1 Cor. 10:10).

15. The aim of these exhortations and warnings is plain. The Philippians are called to set their own house in order so that God's purpose for them as a witnessing community may be fulfilled. This purpose is, first of all, that they *may become blameless and pure.* The verb *become, genēsthe,* is more precisely 'show yourselves'. In view of what has just been written about the internal state of the church, we must find here a call to amendment and improvement by a purging out of the old leaven of party strife and bickering, so that the church may become what it professes to be and ought to be in the intention and service of God.

Blameless, amemptoi, is used by the apostle elsewhere of those to whom he writes (1 Thes. 5:23) and of his own example (1 Thes. 2:10). It means 'irreproachable, living a life at which no finger of criticism may be pointed'. The same word is found in 3:6 of his attainment in the punctilious observance of the ancestral Jewish law; but the point of view, and therefore the meaning, is completely different. In the present context there is no question of human merit; the 'blamelessness' is the work of God in grace (v. 13) and it is set firmly within a social framework, describing the life and character of the church more than the cultivation of individual piety.

Pure, akeraioi is an ethical term used in the Lord's word to his disciples, 'innocent as doves' (Mt. 10:16), and in Romans 16:19, 'innocent about what is evil'. It is employed in first-century literature of wine which is undiluted or metals which contain no weakening alloy: hence 'unmixed, pure'. And there is an interesting use of the word in a Greek version of Canticles 5:2; 6:9 in the description of the Shulamite as 'my dove, my flawless one', 'my perfect one'.

In these combined ethical terms we catch a glimpse of God's

ideal for his people. In their character and conduct there should be no feature on which the outsider would pass a critical verdict, because they see to it that their 'public behaviour is above criticism' (Rom. 12:17, Phillips); and, at the same time, there is no foreign element which intrudes and undermines their strength or contaminates the church's real nature as 'a pure virgin' (2 Cor. 11:2), the bride of Christ. The two words provide an apt commentary on what it means to let our conduct be 'worthy of the gospel of Christ' (1:27).

Paul, however, has more to say on this subject. *Children of God*, as members of his family by adoption and grace are to be *without fault, amōma* (RV, 'without blemish'), set in a hostile world, *a crooked and depraved generation*.

We must look to Deuteronomy 32:5 (RSV) as the source of the apostle's continuing description of the calling and purpose of the church. Of ancient Israel the song of Moses confesses: 'They have dealt corruptly with him (*sic.* God), they are no longer his children (LXX, *tekna*) because of their blemish (LXX, *mōmēta*); they are a perverse and crooked generation (LXX, *genea skolia kai diestrammenē*).' The repetition of words in the Pauline text, *tekna, mōmēta* (which he quotes as *amōma*), *genea skolia kai diestrammenē*, shows that he is quoting from the Old Testament.

But, in adopting this Old Testament indictment of apostate Israel, he also adapts it. He cannot allow that the church has been disinherited and disowned, in spite of its failings and grievous faults. The Philippians are still God's children who are summoned to be 'without blemish', *i.e.* sharing the nature of God whom Moses has described in an earlier verse as 'A God of faithfulness and without iniquity, just and right is he' (Dt. 32:4, RSV). 'His works are perfect', says verse 4, using the Hebrew *tāmim* which in other places underlies the LXX translation *amōmos*, especially when used to describe sacrificial victims as 'without blemish'. Here is a clue to help our understanding of 2:17 which continues the thought of sacrifice and service.

It will be noticed, moreover, that the words *a crooked and depraved generation* are used in Deuteronomy of erring Israel (*cf.* Ps. 78:8); but Paul applies them to the surrounding world in which the church lives and witnesses. It is a hostile world which envelopes the church. It shares with the unbelieving Jews a rejection of the Christian message, and yet its salvation lies only in Christ.

The vocation of believers is to be found and fulfilled *in* (lit. 'in the middle of', *meson*) such a world. The small Greek word *meson* – Paul's insertion into the citation from the LXX – has great significance. Believers in Christ are redeemed out of this present evil world (Gal. 1:4), so that they no longer share its condemnation (1 Cor. 2:6; 7:31; Gal. 6:14), nor its spirit (1 Jn. 2:15–17). They do not belong to the world, to society as alienated from God, indifferent to his presence, and hostile to his rule (see Jn. 17:16); but they are still 'in' the world (Jn. 17:15) and have no mandate to withdraw as recluses and shut themselves away in some secluded place. On the contrary, Christians have a direct commission to go into the world (Jn. 17:18; Mk. 16:15). *In* the world is our proper place as the Lord's people. For it is only there that true Christian witness can be borne and influence for Christ effectively exerted.[1]

The church's influence as a witnessing community is described in the language of the influence of light in a dark place (*cf.* 2 Pet. 1:19). The apostle's thought here is usually taken as referring to stars which shine in a dark firmament: so the Philippians are exhorted to 'shine like stars in a dark world' (Moffatt). To support this rendering Daniel 12:3 (LXX) is quoted: 'and they that are wise shall shine as stars (*hōs phōstēres*) of the heaven'.

But there are cogent objections to this, as Lohmeyer indicates. Paul's verb is *phainesthai*, normally meaning 'to appear', not *phainein*, 'to shine' (as in Dn. 12:3). 'Lights', *phōstēres*, may also mean any object which bears light (*e.g.* torch, lantern, harbour lights[2]). The only other New Testament reference is Revelation 21:11 which describes the holy city as reflecting the glory of God like the light (*phōstēr*) of a jewel. *The universe, kosmos,* which is in view here is not the natural, physical order of creation, but 'the

[1]See, for some attention to the church's calling 'in the world' yet with a distinctive way of life, R. P. Martin, *The Family and the Fellowship: New Testament Images of the Church* (Paternoster/Eerdmans, 1979), pp. 97–111.
[2]So S. K. Finlayson, *ExpT*, 77 (1965–66), p. 181.

world' in its ethical and religious connotation, as when we speak of 'the spirit of the world', or 'worldly people'. Then, there is evidence that Jewish writings spoke of Adam, Israel, the Torah and certain rabbis as 'light-bearers' in the world (*e.g. Test. Levi* 14:3; *cf.* Acts 13:47 quoting Is. 49:6; Rom. 2:19).[1]

The translation 'light-bearers' would be in harmony with Matthew 5:14–16. The disciples are to be the light of the world in the sense that they provide the vessel or vehicle, the lantern, in which the Light of the world (Jn. 8:12) shines forth. In this way Paul's readers are to be seen by the dark world of sin and perversity where they live, as those in whom, like the lampstands of Revelation 1:12, 20, the light of the risen Christ streams forth. They are *children of God*; and also 'the children of light' (1 Thes. 5:5), a title also claimed by the sectarians of the Qumran community (1QS 1.9; 2.16; 1QM 13.5,9).

16. There is no break at this new verse, even if the participle rendered *hold out, epechontes*, is to be construed as an imperative. The Philippians as Christ's 'light-bearers' are, by their example and testimony in the world, to portray *the word of life*. There is some ambiguity in the translation of this phrase. *Epechein* means 'to hold fast or firmly' (Moffatt, RSV) as well as 'to hold out, offer' (AV/KJV, RV, NIV); and the former is to be preferred. The object of the verb is clearly a synonym for the gospel as the word which brings the life of God into the lives of people wherever its message is received and obeyed. See Acts 5:20. This is more likely than a personal reference to Christ as 'the Word of life' (as in 1 Jn. 1:1). The Philippian Christians are to remain firm in their adherence to the truth of the gospel, to hold it fast as a torchbearer would grasp securely the light he carries, and to let no opposition daunt their spirits (see on 1:27). As they do this, they will be discharging their vocation as the true children of God who exercise a potent influence in the midst of the dark and ignorant world which would, if it could, frighten them into fearfulness (1:28) and muffle their clear witness. The two mean-

[1]Strack-Billerbeck, *Kommentar zum N.T.* (Beck, 1922–1956) i, p. 237; iii, p. 357; H. Conzelmann, *TDNT*, 9, pp. 324, 327.

ings of the verb happily dovetail. Only as we firmly 'hold fast' to the gospel truth can we effectively 'hold it out'.

Paul's great pastoral heart is laid bare as at 2 Corinthians 6:11. The Philippians owe it to him as the one through whom they came to believe in the Lord (1 Cor. 3:5) to act upon his directives. Otherwise at the final day of reckoning, *the day of Christ*, they will not be his 'joy and crown' (see on 4:1) and he will then be faced with the sad fact that all his apostolic care and labour will have been *for nothing*. He uses language reminiscent of Isaiah 49:4, where the Servant of the Lord admits, 'I have laboured to no purpose', *kenōs ekopiasa*. The apostle's words of solicitude and trembling fear for his converts (*cf.* Gal. 4:11; 1 Thes. 3:5) are matched, however, by the confidence that his work will not be *for nothing* (*cf.* 1 Cor. 15:58). He trusts that, at the last, he *may boast*, *i.e.* exult at their obedience (2:12) as they heed his direction in the reformation of their church life, the maintenance of their courageous witness in the world and their perseverance unto the end (1:6). Then they, like his other churches, will be his 'crown in which we will glory' (1 Thes. 2:19).

The imagery of the runner in the stadium is to be seen in the words *I did not run*; but as he completes his course he learns that he has been disqualified (1 Cor. 9:27) and, therefore, he has exerted himself needlessly, *for nothing*. So this is his great fear about his apostolic ministry (see Gal. 2:2). Deissmann connects the words *labour for nothing*, *eis kenon ekopiasa*, with Paul's knowledge of weaving, when a piece of cloth would be rejected as badly woven and therefore useless, *eis kenon*.[1] There would be no payment for this! He expresses the hope that it may be otherwise: that he may finish his course with joy (Acts 20:24; *cf.* 2 Tim. 4:7) and that his work may pass the test of the day of Christ and be rewarded (1 Cor. 3:13–14) – these are his confident hopes for his converts.

17. The metaphors of the athletic stadium and the weaver's work-room of the preceding verse are quickly followed by the idiom of sacrifice and ritual. The apostle, in the most solemn

---

[1]Deissmann, *Light from the Ancient East*, p. 317.

personal reference of the whole letter, now sees the prospect of martyrdom for Christ as a very present reality.[1] Yet the scene of the altar and the sacrificial rite is shot through with radiant joy, based on his glad acceptance of God's will for his life. He invites his readers to share that joy in suffering.

There is no point in attempting to minimize the gravity of Paul's words, as Michaelis does (see the Introduction, pp. 35–36). An unfavourable verdict or a change in his fortune will lead to a fateful end: *But even if I am being poured out like a drink offering on the sacrifice and service coming from your faith* . . . Every word here bristles with difficulty, and calls for precise definition. *I am being poured out, spendomai,* is in the present tense and shows that 'the possibility of his execution is vividly present to his own mind' (Michael). Elsewhere he speaks optimistically of release and reunion with the Philippians (see 1:24–26; 2:24), but here it is the sombre reflection of an imminent death which prevails (*cf.* 2 Tim. 4:6 for the same language at the very end of his life). There is, however, the ray of hope as expressed in the fact that the sentence is conditional; but even that is carefully worded. *Alla ei kai, but even if,* is better than 'perhaps' (GNB) or any translation that weakens the note of suggested contingency (*e.g.* AV/KJV and maybe RSV: see later). Kennedy comments that the phrase leaves room for the possibility of death as distinct from *kai ei* which would barely allow the supposition. The verb means 'to pour out as a drink offering' and denotes, in sacrificial terms, a violent, even a bloody, death. He likens his life-blood shed in death to the libation of wine or perfume which was poured out in the concluding rites of a sacrifice to a pagan deity.

The essential part of the sacrificial ritual, however, is not to be found in the libation described by the verb. The real sacrifice is that of the Philippians' *faith.* Paul's libation would not be complete without that and, as Heinzelmann and Bonnard maintain, this act of sacrifice is the main feature of the sentence. They are offering their *faith* in the closeness of their fellowship with the apostle (see on 1:7) and by their active support of his needs (see

---

[1]Against Hawthorne, p. 104–106, who lessens the hazards facing Paul; contrast Motyer, p. 135.

on 4:14). Their gifts, which were sent to him out of their penury (2 Cor. 8:2; *cf.* on 4:19), were a sacrificial service (taking *thysia* and *leitourgia* as one phrase, governed by one definite article) which was acceptable to God as 'a fragrant offering' (4:18).

This train of thought continues the reference made in verse 15 to the Philippians as 'blameless'. The epithet is applied to sacrificial animals which must be unmarked and in perfect condition to be used in the Hebrew ritual (see Lv. 1:10; 22:17–25; 1 Pet. 1:19; *cf.* Heb. 9:14). It is possible, therefore, that it may be the Old Testament cultus of sacrifice that the apostle had in mind in his earlier allusion to the drink-offering (*cf.* Nu. 15:1–10; 28:7 though Collange and Hawthorne make the point that the verb 'to be poured out' does not necessarily connote an offering in blood, *i.e.* involving the death of the victim). In this case the preposition *on, epi,* must carry the meaning 'in addition to', 'to the accompaniment of' because, in Jewish sacrifices, the libation was poured out near or around the altar and not actually on the victim (*cf.* Josephus, *Antiquities*, 3.9, 4).

The conclusion then may be stated. The Philippians are spoken of as exercising their priestly ministry of service to God (*cf.* Rom. 12:1; 1 Pet. 2:5). Their *faith*, made visible and evident in the gifts which they had sacrificially contributed and which gave them a share in Paul's affliction (4:14), is the sacrifice (so exactly Heb. 13:16). Paul's life-blood, to be shed (so he fears) in martyrdom for Christ, is the accompanying libation. It is important to see that *I am being poured out* is a verb in the passive voice and figurative in meaning. Paul is not offering anything, whether his own life or the Philippians' faith, as some read this verse (*e.g.* Michaelis and, similarly, Dodd and Grayston). Michaelis makes the offering of Paul's missionary activity the cultic service in the interest of the Philippians' faith, quoting Romans 15:16. But this view is not so acceptable as the one given above. Nor is Hawthorne's interpretation that Paul is 'picturesquely referring to his sufferings as an apostle', not his violent death in prospect, any more convincing in view of 2 Timothy 4:6 and the strong adversative at the head of the verse. Philippians 1:15–26 confirms that a more serious exigency is in his mind's eye as he writes.

The apostle's outlook, as he stands before the prospect of a martyr's crown, is that of joy (*I am glad and rejoice*). Such an unexpected reaction is no morbid yearning for death as in the case of Ignatius some years later. He uses a cognate form of Paul's verb implying martyrdom but with a different conception of death: 'Grant me nothing more than to be poured out (*spondisthēnai*) to God' (*Rom.* 2:2). With Paul his joy is based on a confidence that death is gain because by it Christ is magnified and the gospel proclaimed (see on 1:21). He rejoices equally with his friends at Philippi in their sacrifice on his behalf.

18. The phrase *to de auto kai*, *so (you) too* simply repeats the thought of the preceding verse. This is a call to the readers to receive the news he has just given them with gladness, and to share his joy.

The two verses, 17–18, present a memorable picture of the joy which Paul was experiencing in his confinement and, at the same time, endeavouring to inculcate in the Philippians. Also they tell us much about the intimacy of Christian sympathy and fellow-feeling which is marked throughout the letter. The prefix of the verb *rejoice*, *synchairō* in verse 17, *synchairete* in verse 18, is characteristic. *Syn*, translated here *with* is the preposition of united experience. It is used to underline the importance of unity within the church as all divisions are cancelled out (1:27). It betokens, too, the close bond between the apostle and the church (*cf.* 1:7) and between the apostle and certain individuals in the church (2:25; 4:3). Above all, the Philippians have proved that the link between them and Paul was reciprocal by their ready material help (4:14).

VI. FUTURE PLANS (2:19–30)

A. THE COMMENDATION OF TIMOTHY (2:19–24)

The subject-matter of the letter changes at this point as Paul expresses his hopes for the future and his intention to send Timothy on a goodwill mission to Philippi. These plans (called a 'travelogue'[1] to denote what Paul had in intention, notably his desire to visit his congregations as a follow-up to his letters) are stated in carefully phrased language which provides us with some valuable clues to the outstanding problem of the epistle which Deissmann has described as 'the circumstances in which' the letter was written, 'the journeys that must be presupposed, and other external events in the lives of the apostle and his companions'.[2]

19. 'But' (*de*; not in NIV) marks the link with verse 12. The apostle has already referred to this unavoidable absence which was caused by his enforced captivity. But he is concerned about the Philippians' welfare. So he will send Timothy, who was his companion at this time (see 1:1), as his envoy and representative. He is hopeful that the report which his younger colleague will bring back will be satisfactory and that he *may be cheered when I receive news about you*. The mission of Timothy will therefore be a powerful follow-up to the appeals to unity and steadfastness which are the burden of his letter. For Timothy as Paul's personal representative to the churches see 1 Corinthians 4:17; 16:10 and 1 Thessalonians 3:2.

The importance of this proposed journey against the background of the apostle's own unsettled and even precarious future as a prisoner is underscored by the phrase *in the Lord Jesus*. Hawthorne's 'under the lordship of Jesus' is an unusual translation, but suggestive. It incidentally supports my view of 2:5–11. Nowhere else in the other references to his proposed journeys does he use this phrase (*cf.* Rom. 15:24; 1 Cor. 16:7; 2 Cor. 13:2; 1 Tim. 3:14; Phm. 22); and this fact cannot, as Lohmeyer points out, be accidental. There is more in the use of the phrase here than simply his instinct to refer all things to his union with his Lord. At a time of crisis and tension when the outlook is unsettled and he does not know what a day may

---

[1]See Doty, *Letters in Primitive Christianity*, p. 43, who gives a useful chart of such plans.
[2]See Deissmann, *Light from the Ancient East*, pp. 238, 239. J. L. White, *The Form and Function of the Body of the Greek Letter: A Study of the Letter-Body in the Non-Literary Papyri and in Paul the Apostle* (Scholars Press, 1972), pp. 143 ff., has pertinent comment to update Deissmann's discussion.

bring forth he can only make his plans *in the Lord Jesus* or 'in the Lord' (see on v. 24). This means that his hopes are governed by the Lord's will for his situation, and equally that his plans do not rest on a human calculation of release and freedom. They are based on God's undertaking for him. (See the Introduction, p. 36.)

The purpose of Timothy's visit is expressed by the words *that I also may be cheered*. The pronoun *I* is emphatic, and is preceded by *kai*, translated by *also*. The force of this construction is: 'not only will you be encouraged to have firsthand news of me here, I too shall be heartened when I get news of you at Philippi on Timothy's return'. So two journeys are in view in one sentence: Timothy's to Philippi and his reporting back to Paul's prison.

The verb *eupsychein* is found only here in the New Testament. It is absent from the LXX and rare in classical and Hellenistic Greek, but is frequently used as a sepulchral inscription with the sense, 'Farewell, may it be well with your soul'. The imperative *eupsychei* here represents a pious wish for the departed. From this usage Lohmeyer raises the possibility that Paul may have his own approaching death in view. Against this, however, it is clear that he expects to be alive to receive news of the Philippians on Timothy's return, hence his use of the first personal singular subjunctive *eupsychō, that I also may be cheered*; but there is a note of uncertainty about his future in verse 23.

20. Timothy's value as a trusted colleague is commended. *I have no-one else like him* (lit. 'of equal soul') is a tribute of high praise from the apostle, and puts Timothy in a very honoured position as a key man on whom Paul depended. The adjective here, *isopsychos*, is cognate with 'be cheered' in the previous verse, and like that word is extremely rare. Indeed Dibelius takes the two terms as an intended word-play, as though Paul were deliberately employing unfamiliar words, and one rare term suggests another. The LXX of Psalm 55:13 (54:14), 'a man mine equal', shows that it is used of close human friendship. The sense of the passage seems to be that of all his Christian friends in the place of his confinement, *i.e.* the brethren who are with him (4:21) and 'the saints' and members of Caesar's household (4:22), there is no-one who shares so intimately Timothy's deep concern for the Philippians. The alternative translation (*e.g.* by Collange: 'he is the only one who truly shares my preoccupations')[1] founders on the fact that Paul's Greek construction cannot mean that he is referring to himself, because if that had been in his mind he must have written, 'I have no-one *else* like myself'.[2] So Gnilka, Beare, Michael, Wilson.

He has no-one of the same spirit as Timothy and this fact makes him Paul's right-hand man for the Philippians' situation. He will take(s) *a genuine interest in your welfare, i.e.* have a genuine interest in and concern for your churchly wellbeing. The token of this painstaking interest in them is seen in Paul's choice of him when someone was required to undertake the journey. If, however, the next verse is to be taken as part of the same situation, the thought could be that he was the only one found willing to go to Philippi.

The adverb translated as an adjective *genuine, gnēsiōs* (*cf.* 4:3), recalls Timothy's relationship to Paul as his 'true (*gnēsios*) son in the faith' (1 Tim. 1:2). Comparing 2 Corinthians 11:28 we see how deeply he had drunk of the apostle's spirit and attitude to his missionary and pastoral work. 'My concern for all the churches' was shared by both men. There is no contradiction here with 4:6 or 1 Corinthians 7:32. What is forbidden there is anxious care for one's self and one's own interests. Timothy's 'anxiety' was for the spiritual welfare of others.

In Christian experience it is remarkable how often these apparent contradictions go together, but in reverse. We find ourselves guilty of anxiety over our own interests to the exclusion of others' wellbeing. One of the surest antidotes to personal 'care' is to widen our horizons and so enlarge our heart of sympathy that we share the burdens of other people. So 1 Corinthians 12:25 states our Christian responsibility for other believers, using the identical verb, *merimnaō*.[3]

---

[1]*Cf.* Caird, Houlden, Hawthorne, P. Christou, *JBL*, 70, 1951, pp. 293–296.

[2]Another rendering supplies the pronoun *hymin*, 'with you', and gives the sense 'having much in common with you'. Timothy stands out on account of his unique appreciation of the Philippians themselves. See BAGD, *s.v. isopsychos*.

[3]See the treatment of the word in Martin, *The Spirit and the Congregation*, pp. 29, 30.

21. Does this verse represent the apostle's bitter complaint that, when he sought a fellow-believer to go to Philippi, there was none forthcoming because they were 'wrapped up in their own affairs' and did 'not really care for the business of Jesus Christ' (Phillips)? Is he here, as Michael says, 'guilty of ungracious petulance' and, at the same time, prone to exaggerate by the sweeping indictment of *everyone, hoi pantes* (*i.e.* one and all, all without exception), who are bent on their own ways? The mood of the sentence may reflect the enmity and division which has been aroused in the local church of the place where he was (see on 1:15–18); but even then it is necessary to suppose that, if the verse is taken at its face-value, there was literally no other Christian, apart from Timothy, upon whom he could count at this time. In the Corinthian crisis Paul felt bereft of all human support (2 Cor. 1:8; 4:7–12); and this judgment may be directed to his detractors at Corinth (2 Cor. 11:1 – 12:13). The allusion to his rivals in 1:17 may be connected similarly.

There are other possibilities, however. Paul may mean that of all the Christians around him, there was no-one to whom he can entrust so important a mission. There may have been good and loyal persons within call but Paul has not asked them to be his ambassadors to Philippi because they lack the right qualities and disposition. The sentence then becomes not a sweeping criticism but a sorrowful, matter-of-fact statement that there is no-one else capable of a duty which required certain gifts and graces. But this view hardly does justice to the incisive words of the text.

Alternatively, we may submit that the sentence is really an aside. It is Paul's general comment, in parenthesis, on the state of the world around him. The sentence is crisp and pointed as such a comment, an *obiter dictum*, should be. It says nothing about his fellow-Christians; but it is rather his solemn reflection when he remembers that, in a world of selfishness and self-seeking (*cf.* Rom. 5:7 for a parallel reflection), it is such a rare thing to find a man like Timothy who is really anxious to promote the welfare of other people, and to give himself to a fatiguing journey and to the resolving of personal quarrels in the Philippian church. This would be a delicate issue to handle, calling for tact, wisdom and patience. No-one with any pastoral experience would deny that Timothy's task will be unenviable; and especially for a young man (1 Tim. 4:12), physically weak (1 Tim. 5:23) and temperamentally reserved (1 Cor. 16:10). His readiness to help, then, supremely exemplifies a selfless, altruistic spirit unlike that described in 2:1–4. Contrast 1 Corinthians 10:24; 13:5 where the same verb 'seek', *zēteō*, is used.

22. Not only does Timothy enjoy Paul's fullest confidence and approval; to the Philippians also he is *persona grata*. *You know that Timothy has proved himself* really means, 'You know how he has stood the test and shown himself to be a man of sound character and worthiness.' Since the time of Paul's first visit to their city (Acts 16), when Timothy accompanied the apostle, they had known of his close association with God's servant in his apostolic labours. This acquaintance with his career would confirm to them that his testing in the hard school of missionary travels and vicissitudes had been thorough and complete. *Proved* is really a noun (*dokimē*) and is related to the verb 'approve' in 1:10 (see note there). Timothy had been tested and approved.

Furthermore, the record of his companionship with Paul in the work of the gospel is described in the intimate terms of the parent-child relationship. *As a son with his father* points to this connection between preacher and convert (see Paul's use of the same idea in 1 Cor. 4:14–15; Phm. 10; *cf.* Gal. 4:19; 1 Thes. 2:11). Paul was his father in the gospel, leading him to Christ and fostering him in the things of the Lord (Acts 16:1–3; 1 Tim. 4:14; 2 Tim. 1:6), as 'my son whom I love' (1 Cor. 4:17). Filial obedience was a very real duty in the first century, and this is brought out in the strong verb *has served*, *edouleusen*, lit. 'served as a slave'. But Paul does not actually say that Timothy served him as a slave. Rather he skilfully turns the sentence in another direction as he was probably arrested by the thought that he, no less than Timothy, was a slave of Jesus Christ (1:1). He writes, then, 'he served *with* me as a slave for the extension of the gospel'. On the phrase *in the work of the gospel, eis to euangelion,* see 1:5 and the Introduction, p. 49.

Paul and Timothy are yoked together in common service for a single cause, *the gospel* (see the Introduction, pp. 52–53). This almost incidental allusion to Paul's junior colleague provides a reminder that, in the church of God, the only claim to position and honour is based on service to the cause of him who came to take the form of a slave (2:7).

23. After the commendation of Timothy there comes the apostle's hope that he will be able to send him *soon, exautēs, i.e.* immediately. But this promise is modified by the clause *as soon as I see how things go with me.* As soon as Paul has clear knowledge of what is to be the outcome of his detention (so Gnilka) he will send Timothy to them. Then Timothy will be able to bring news either of Paul's condemnation or his release. At the moment when the letter is dispatched there is no certain news about his future.

This verse militates against a dating of the epistle during Paul's confinement at Caesarea (Acts 23:33ff.), as Kennedy remarks and Hawthorne ignores, adding – quite gratuitously – that Paul was merely awaiting 'the final verdict of acquittal handed down by the governor'. Caird's statement is more secure: Paul 'cannot have had much confidence in his release, or would not have needed to send Timothy'; and equally it is destructive of the view that Paul had such plans while he was a prisoner at Rome, according to Acts 28:30–31, unless we suppose a number of events which are not recorded in the book of Acts (*e.g.* Timothy's presence in Rome, and a change of plan in regard to his resumption of apostolic work in the east). See the Introduction under section II. On an earlier dating the mission of Timothy referred to in the present verse will be that of Acts 19:22.

24. The outcome of his incarceration is uncertain (1:22–23) so what he hopes for is prefaced by the knowledge that it is only *in the Lord* that he can look ahead with confidence. The same hesitation which may be detected elsewhere in the letter (see on

1:20–26; 2:19) is found again in this phrase. If he has any assurance of a happy issue out of his troubles it is only in submission to the divine will, and therefore *in the Lord* may be the equivalent of 'if the Lord is willing', as in 1 Corinthians 4:19.

On the other hand, it may mean that if he is to escape death it will only be the result of divine intervention (*cf.* 2 Cor. 1:9–10 for parallel thought, or possibly these verses refer to the same incident). The strong verb *I am confident, pepoitha*, endorses this latter view. The situation, then, is this: Paul awaits the judges' verdict. When that is known he will commission Timothy to make the journey to Philippi. If the verdict goes against him, Timothy as Paul's envoy will act in the apostle's name as one sent 'in the Lord Jesus' (v. 19). If, however, it is a favourable decision and brings release from his chains Paul will follow 'shortly' (RSV), *i.e.* soon after Timothy or maybe 'certainly' (*i.e.* he will keep his promise: this sense of *tacheōs* is seen in Rev. 22:20).

Here again the book of Acts is silent about a release from Roman imprisonment and we know nothing of a renewal of contact with Philippi. On the earlier dating of the letter, however, the promised visit was realized in Acts 20:1–6. See Introduction, pp. 25, 32.

B. THE COMMENDATION OF EPAPHRODITUS (2:25–30)

The apostle turns from considering his future plans to the immediate present, and in this he is concerned to commend Epaphroditus to the Philippian church. It is uncertain whether this man was still with Paul when he wrote the epistle or had already begun his journey back to Philippi. Most commentators take the former view, and describe him as the bearer of the letter to the church, although C. O. Buchanan[1] finds indications (*e.g.* in vv. 26–27) that he had already left Paul's company and had either returned to his native city or was on his way there.

---

[1]Buchanan, *EQ*, 36, 1964, pp. 157–166.

25. Assuming that *Epaphroditus* was to be the bearer of the letter, the tense of 'I have thought it necessary to send' (RSV) must be taken as 'epistolary aorist', *i.e.* the writer puts himself in the position of the reader for whom, when he reads the letter, the writer's present actions and thoughts will be past. The above translation suggests this but NIV opts for the present tense: *But I think it is necessary to send back*, which is more in accord with modern usage. Notice too the insertion of 'send *back*', which is not in the Greek. See below.

Epaphroditus, which means 'charming', is a common name in ancient inscriptions. He is not the same as the Epaphras of Colossians 1:7; 4:12, although, in the original Greek, the latter is an abbreviated form of the first name. The apostle speaks, in glowing terms, of the value of Epaphroditus' companionship. He has been *my brother*, *i.e.* a fellow-believer, *and fellow-worker*, *i.e.* in the same service for the kingdom of God. This phrase represents one Greek word, *synergos*, and possibly looks back to Epaphroditus' early association with Paul in the days when the Philippian church was established. It may also refer to his partnership in the gospel at the place of Paul's confinement (*cf.* 4:3). *Fellow-soldier* recalls the sense of camaraderie which bound the two men in the conflict, both at Philippi and in the apostle's present situation (*cf.* Phm. 2).

Special mention is made of the service which this valued colleague of the apostle had rendered (*cf.* v. 30). He had come to Paul in the name of the church whose *messenger* (lit. 'apostle') he was, to bring the money gift as the expression of its partnership in the gospel (see notes on 1:5 and 4:18). It seems clear, also, that it was the intention of the Philippians (and his own, too) that he should stay indefinitely as companion to Paul, although some suppose that he intended to return after the completion of his mission. But the language of verses 25 and 28 seems decisively against this view: in both the verb is *send*, not 'send back'. He had come to Paul to remain with him.

The picture of Epaphroditus as the authorized representative of a community, in this case the Philippian church, corresponds with one of the meanings of the Hebrew *shaliach* (see also 2 Cor. 8:23). This term underlies the word *apostolos* here, which is not used in this place in any technical sense but rather carrying the thought of John 13:16, 'he that is sent'.

Having handed over the gift to Paul, Epaphroditus stayed on and assisted Paul: so *whom you sent to take care of my needs*. The NIV translates a noun, *leitourgos*, 'servant', which, in first-century literature, conveys associations of sacred and solemn work undertaken for religious purposes. Paul uses the word of himself in Romans 15:16, and of the work of the collection for the Jerusalem poor in Romans 15:27 and 2 Corinthians 9:12. (*Cf.* 2:17 for a further use of the same root word.) Such service is thus invested with an aura of special solemnity, and Paul views it as rendered to the Lord, as well as to himself.

26. The fine plans of the Philippians in the visit and ministration of Epaphroditus had gone awry. Unhappily he had fallen ill either en route to see Paul (Caird, Bruce) or when he arrived; somehow news of this sickness had travelled to Philippi, and from there a report had come back to Paul that the Philippians were concerned about him. We observe again the double journey involved. This, in turn, reacted upon Epaphroditus who was in great distress, which is marked by two strong terms, *longs for all of you, epipothōn*, and *is distressed, adēmonōn*. For the first word see note on 1:8, where it is used of Paul's ardent desire to see the Philippians once more. The second term is used to describe the Lord's agony in Gethsemane (Mt. 26:37; Mk. 14:33), and denotes great mental and spiritual perturbation. It denotes a 'confused, restless, half-distracted state' (Lightfoot) for which 'very upset' (GNB) is hardly adequate.

We can only guess at the nature of his sickness, a term which could cover a nervous disorder as well as bodily suffering. Possibly the tension of the imprisonment was too great an ordeal for him. We can, however, affirm that it was directly connected with the work of Christ (v. 30); that it was brought about by his visit to Paul and the service he rendered him as a prisoner (v. 30); and that it was a source of great disquiet to the apostle no less than to the Philippians themselves (vv. 27–28).

Epaphroditus' longing for his native city and a restoration to his Christian friends there has been variously interpreted as homesickness (a possible meaning of *distressed*), or, if he were a leader in the church, a pastoral solicitude for the 'flock' from which he was separated or, more likely, a desire to be back home in order to defend Paul's gospel at Philippi. Lohmeyer, with his theory of the Philippian church as a persecuted community, takes Epaphroditus' yearning for his fellow-believers as a sign of his desire to aid them in their struggle against the enemies of the gospel.

27. Paul writes to reassure his readers that Epaphroditus' sickness is now over and, by the mercy of God, their delegate has recovered. This is the natural meaning of *God had mercy on him*. This divine mercy is shown elsewhere in restoring the sick in mind and body (as in Mk. 5:19), and in consoling the anxious (2 Cor. 1:3ff.). Both the sick Philippian and the concerned apostle have known this gracious work of God in their lives. If these words are intended to convey the apostle's reassurance that all is well, it is scarcely likely that Epaphroditus had already returned home, but it is just possible that he was on his way homeward when Paul wrote these words.

The sickness must have been grave. The sick man was *in extremis*, he *almost died*. Compare the similar phrase in verse 30 which is used also of the Saviour's death on the cross in 2:8. But there is no vital connection between the sentences as has been suggested. Indeed, unlike the suffering Lord of Calvary, Epaphroditus had been rescued from the brink of the grave by God's tender pity. His life had been spared (contrast Rom. 8:32), whether by answer to prayer or the use of medicines, or a doctor's services, Paul does not say. 'What concerns the apostle is not the healing itself, but its significance' (Collange). At the same time, Paul's lot had been eased; for if Epaphroditus had died, the sorrow of bereavement would have been added to the misery of the apostle's imprisonment. *Sorrow upon sorrow* reflects some great despair which had settled upon God's servant and of which 2 Corinthians 1:8ff. is taken by some commentators to be an indication. (See the Introduction, p. 30.)

28. Paul resumes the statement of his immediate plan. *I am all the more eager* renders a comparative adverb (*spoudaioterōs*) that can be taken as a superlative as in 2 Corinthians 8:17. It is better to translate, therefore: 'I am very eagerly sending . . .', for the verb in Greek (*epempsa*, lit. 'I sent'), is again probably epistolary (as in v. 25), unless Epaphroditus had already departed for home.

His return to Philippi is to be attended by joy on the part of the brethren there; and the apostle inserts the following commendation to avoid any suspicion of criticism against the church's ambassador, and to make it clear that he accepts full responsibility for the decision that Epaphroditus should return (v. 25). This unexpected return may have caused great disappointment in the church, and have led some to conclude that his mission had failed, and that Paul had been bereft of sympathetic human friendship at an hour when he needed it most (see 2:20-21). Paul would answer that criticism in advance by a glowing appraisal of the worth of their leader, and a record of the circumstances which led to his departure homeward. Not only should they forbear from fault-finding, they should *be glad* that he had been restored to health and is to be with them once again.

Less anxiety is again a window into the apostle's 'struggle' (see 1:30) at the scene of his imprisonment. The sorrow which he endures would only be intensified if he came to hear that Epaphroditus had been attacked as a deserter and a weakling. He feels that, as it is right for their messenger to return, so the Philippians too must accept this as a providential ordering of the situation and a divine overruling of their plans.

29. Epaphroditus is to be welcomed *in the Lord with great joy*. If *in the Lord* is to be taken with the verb it may mean, 'as the Lord would receive him' (*cf.* Rom. 15:7); or, if the phrase qualifies *with great joy* the sense will be, 'with unalloyed pleasure which characterizes a welcome in the church of Christ' as at the Lord's table or with practical hospitality.[1]

---

[1]Getty, p. 46.

Romans 16:2 is parallel to this second usage. Ideally both these interpretations should mean the same thing. Our attitude to fellow-Christians, especially when the tendency to misunderstand their motives and to malign their actions has to be resisted, should be the attitude of the Lord himself to us. He has received us in love; and love is 'always eager to believe the best' (1 Cor. 13:7, Moffatt). Or else *in the Lord* depicts the quality of life befitting those who are 'in Christ' (as in 2:5). So Collange.

With this appeal to greet their returning delegate in royal fashion there goes a memorable eulogy of his character and sterling worth. Literally the apostle's appeal reads, 'Hold such men as valuable', *entimous*, (NIV *honour men like him*), for the reason given in the next verse.

30. Epaphroditus had faced suffering and death *for the work of Christ*. Although only one MS reads simply 'the work', many commentators accept this shortened form (*cf.* Acts 15:38), following Lightfoot. Other MSS read 'the work of the Lord', but this, like the NIV, seems to be an insertion to explain the original simple form.

Many MSS have the participle *paraboleusamenos* with the meaning 'hazarding his life'; this preferred reading is reflected in the NIV, *risking his life*, over against a variant with an extra Greek letter (*parabouleusamenos*) which AV/KJV accepts and renders, 'not regarding his life'. This is illustrated by Deissmann, who quotes an inscription found at Olba on the Black Sea, dated at the end of the second century, in honour of a certain Carzoazus who 'exposed himself to dangers (*paraboleusamenos*) as an advocate in (legal) strife (by taking his clients' cases even) up to (*mechri*) the emperors (Augustus and Tiberius)'.[1]

This reading gives a better meaning, and is accepted by modern editors generally. It is a gambling term. Epaphroditus staked his life for the service of Christ, in the interest of the apostle and on behalf of the Philippian community whose lack of help was unavoidable since they were miles away. Such a word brings its own challenge and rebuke to an easy-going Christianity which

---

[1]Deissmann, *Light from the Ancient East*, p. 88 and notes.

makes no stern demands, and calls for no limits of self-denying, self-effacing sacrifice. Here is a man who gave little thought to personal comfort and safety in order to discharge his responsibility; and we cannot accept Michaelis' rather uncharitable suggestion that he may have acted in a specially foolhardy way and brought harm upon himself.

There is no touch of harshness or mention of complaint concerning the Philippians as the text *to make up for the help you could not give me* might suggest. The thought has a parallel in 1 Corinthians 16:17, where the coming of Stephanas, Fortunatus and Achaicus make up for the absence of the Corinthians. This service, *leitourgia*, was the ministry of the gospel in which Paul and the Philippians were unitedly engaged. They shared in it (see on 1:5) by their gift, and actively in the person of Epaphroditus who, as their 'messenger' and '*leitourgos* of my need' (v. 25), laboured side by side with the apostle.

VII. WARNINGS AND ENCOURAGEMENTS (3:1-21)

A. PAUL'S WARNING AND CLAIM (3:1-3)

1. The phrase *Finally (to loipon), my brothers* would lead us to expect the conclusion of the letter; but this is not the case, and the apostle has occasion to renew the promise of a conclusion in 4:8, after much intervening discussion. In any case, *to loipon* could just as well be rendered 'Well, then' (Hawthorne) 'Furthermore' or 'To proceed, then' (Motyer), with no thought of 'In conclusion' (GNB, JB) or 'farewell' (NEB). The call to *rejoice in the Lord* is a characteristic phrase in the epistle, repeated at 4:4. *In the Lord* may signify 'because you are the Lord's', or 'because of what he has done', or the entire phrase may be the Christian equivalent of the Old Testament exclamation, *Hallelujah*, 'Praise the Lord', which is familiar to us in the Psalter. Moffatt's translation takes this encouragement to *rejoice in the Lord* as explaining *the same things* which are left undefined in the passage. The fact that the apostle writes about these things makes it clear that they can hardly be oral instructions given earlier to the church.[1] We may also note that Paul does not hesitate (this is the real meaning of *it is no trouble*[2]) to repeat these things as a safe course for his readers. The following explanations of this enigmatic phrase *to write the same things to you again* have been offered.

1. Moffatt's 'I am repeating this word "rejoice" in my letter' boldly connects the phrase with the exhortation to rejoice. This has something to support it, and when Michael, who rejects it, says that 'while it is true that the note of joy is sounded throughout the epistle, not until we come to 3:1a do we find a direct injunction to rejoice', he has overlooked 2:18; and this text could possibly contain the call which is renewed in 3:1a. The one objection is that, as Lightfoot says, 'such an injunction has no very direct bearing on the *safety* of the Philippians'. (So Bruce too.) But their succumbing to depression and despondency under trial may have seemed to Paul a very real danger. NIV follows this view by adding *again*, a word not represented in the Greek text.

2. *The same things* may be, as Lightfoot held, an allusion to the repeated warnings against dissensions within the church. This word of caution is picked up at 4:1ff., which Lightfoot regards as following on closely from the injunction of 3:1, with the intervening verses of chapter 3 as a digression caused by an interruption in the apostle's thought.

3. Michael and Beare suppose that verses 1a–9 form part of a separate Pauline letter, not addressed to Philippi, and therefore we have no clue as to what *the same things* mean. See the Introduction, pp. 38–40.

4. There may be a looking forward at this juncture to the following warnings against the enemies of the gospel (given in vv. 2ff.). This gives an excellent introduction to what follows. Paul does not hesitate to take up the vital matter of warning the Philippians against false teachers. He has possibly sent previous messages of warning in letters which are now lost; now he

[1]V. P. Furnish, *NTS*, 10, 1963, 80–83.
[2]Dibelius regards the Greek words *ouk oknēron*, RSV, 'not irksome', as equivalent to a stylistic formula *ouk oknō*, 'I do not shrink from', and to refer back to the preceding appeal to joy in 2:28–29.

reiterates the teaching. Such repeated warnings are necessary for their well-being, *it is a safeguard for you*. This is the view taken by Kennedy, Scott, Benoit and Getty. It may well have been a report of danger which the apostle knew to be approaching the Philippian church that prompted him to embark upon the long section of the chapter. See further in the Introduction, p. 41.

2. The tone of the letter changes unexpectedly at this point. See the Introduction, pp. 38–41. The threefold warning is couched in strong, vigorous language with the repetition of the verb in the imperative mood, *blepete*, 'look out for', 'be warned against', betraying something of the tense earnestness and emphasis of a serious warning. It is not quite 'consider' in a neutral light. It is not probable that distinct and different classes are meant as Synge supposes. Paul has one hostile group in mind, and describes it in three ways: *dogs . . . men who do evil . . . mutilators of the flesh*.

To identify the persons who are so described, the choice is between Jews and Jewish Christians. Both were a constant thorn in the flesh of the apostle. 2 Corinthians 11:13 speaks of the opponents as 'deceitful workmen', and points to the same identification here. Against the opinion that the Jews are in mind is the way in which circumcision is derisively spoken of as 'cutting' (NIV *mutilators*) and the argument against circumcision is noticeably absent from 2 Corinthians where Paul's adversaries are a type of itinerant missionary of Jewish origin (2 Cor. 11:22), who displayed a forceful presence and challenged Paul's lowly person. Paul speaks respectfully of the Jewish rite as practised by the Jews (Rom. 2:25; 3:1–2; 15:8; Col. 4:11; *cf.* Phil. 3:5), but what did infuriate him was the insistence that the rite must be enforced on Gentile Christians in order to make them 'full Christians', as the Judaizers required (Acts 15:1). Against such a false doctrine and conception of circumcision he writes trenchantly to the Galatians (5:2ff.).

The charge levelled against the teachers whose activities were an imminent danger to the community at Philippi is expressed in fierce terms. *Dogs* were regarded by the Jews as 'the most despised, insolent and miserable' of creatures[1] and as unclean (Mt. 15:26; Rev. 22:15). It was a derogatory title used by orthodox Jews for the Gentile nations who were treated as Israel's enemies and therefore God's (Enoch 89:42). In the present verse the application is reversed and the enemies of God are now those Jewish Christian emissaries who misrepresent the gospel (2 Cor. 11:3–4, 13–15) and thereby put themselves under the ban of God (2 Cor. 11:15b; *cf. Didache* 9:5, quoting Mt. 7:6; Ignatius, *To the Ephesians*, 7:1, where he describes heretical teachers as 'mad dogs'). Possibly, however, it was not the disgrace of the false leaders, or their impudence, as Dibelius suggests, which Paul had in mind so much as their incessant, dog-like yelping (Ps. 59:6, 14) as they untiringly 'dog' his footsteps, and try to 'worry' him in his work.

Men who do evil corresponds with the same description as in 2 Corinthians 11:13. In both cases, if the accent is put on 'workers', *ergatai*, there may be an ironical exposure of their constant harping on the necessity of 'works' to secure salvation. This 'confidence in the flesh' (v. 4), *i.e.* trust in self-acquired merit through religious and moral practices, comes in for stern condemnation in Galatians and Romans, but for somewhat different reasons.

Those mutilators of the flesh refers to the practice of circumcision; but Paul will not give it its proper name *peritomē*. Instead, by a pun, he mockingly calls it a mere cutting, *katatomē*, *i.e.* mutilation of the body on a par with pagan practices forbidden in Leviticus 21:5 (*cf.* 1 Ki. 18:28, and the frenzied rituals of the devotees of Cybele, described in Lucian's *The Ass* and Apuleius' *Golden Ass*).[2] The same derision is applied to the Judaizers in Galatians 5:12, where *apokoptein*, 'to cut off' is a reference to their concern with the physical act of circumcision, and ironically means also 'to castrate'.

---

[1] *Cf.* Strack-Billerbeck, i, pp. 722–725.
[2] See description in T. R. Glover, *The Conflict of Religions in the Early Roman Empire* (Methuen, 1910), pp. 20, 21.

3. The true name *peritomē* is served for Christians who are the circumcision which, in the light of Romans 2:25–29 and Colossians 2:11, must be a title for the church as the covenant people of God inheriting all the promises made to ancient Israel (Rom. 9:24–26; 1 Pet. 2:9–10). The term *circumcision* changes its meaning according to the context. Here, as Dibelius says, 'the thought is not that of a bodily mark but of the church's consciousness of being the new people of God'. For the original application of the word to the Jews, Israel 'after the flesh', *cf.* Galatians 2:7–9, 12. The Christian church, however, composed of believing Jews and Gentiles, is the new Israel, 'the Israel of God' (Gal. 6:16), and so can be styled *the circumcision* because the term is given a new, spiritual and inner content (so, clearly, Rom. 2:28–29); and its value derives directly from its new meaning. Otherwise it is meaningless (Gal. 5:6; 6:15), and if practised literally, in unbelief, positively ruinous (Gal. 5:2–4). This verdict on the Jewish rite as applied to Gentile believers is based on the Jewish Christian claim to a righteousness by ceremony which Paul opposes, and on the perpetuating of a distinction within the church between Jew and Gentile, which he denies (Gal. 3:26–29; Col. 3:11).

There are prophetic indications in the Old Testament and at Qumran (Lv. 26:41, Dt. 10:16; Je. 4:4; 1QS 5:5, 26; *cf. Barnabas*, 9) and suggestions in Philo that the physical rite as a badge of membership of the elect nation was not enough. The true circumcision is a spiritual work, and for Christian believers is pictured in the symbolism of baptism (Col. 2:11–13). Nothing could be clearer than the way in which the Old Testament ritual gives way to the New Testament insistence on the inner significance of personal response to God, while at the same time the value of ordinances is retained and invested with a deeper meaning than a merely outward act (such as circumcision).

Over against Jewish formalism there are set forth three affirmations of Christian status and privilege. *Worship by the Spirit of God* makes plain the intensely spiritual character of Christian worship according to our Lord's teaching (Jn. 4:24). Whatever outward forms and ceremonies may or may not be used, nothing can detract from the indispensable qualification, 'in spirit and in truth', which should be the dominating feature of worship, and the equally important 'broken and contrite heart' (Ps. 51:17) of the individual worshipper. It is the Holy Spirit of God who alone can inspire such worship; and every time we assemble for the noblest of all occupations, the worship of the Lord our God, we ought prayerfully to acknowledge this, and to remind ourselves of our complete dependence upon him.[1]

Another distinctive mark of 'the Israel of God' is that its members *glory in Christ Jesus*. It is better to render *kauchōmenoi* as 'exult' (as in 1:26; 2:16; *cf.* Rom. 5:2; 1 Cor. 1:31; 2 Cor. 10:17). It is almost impossible to list all the references to this verb which is clearly a favourite one of Paul's. It occurs some thirty-five times in his writings and only twice elsewhere in the New Testament. It is used chiefly to define two extremes of religious attitude; either proud self-confidence (*e.g.* Gal. 6:13), or humble submission to God's grace as revealed in the cross of Jesus (*e.g.* Gal. 6:14). In origin the term goes back to Jeremiah 9:23–24 (*cf.* 1 Cor. 1:31).

The exultation of the believer in the Saviour stems from, and is based on, his finished work. Our 'boasting' is not in ourselves, which is the essence of sin, but in another whose arm alone has brought salvation and on whom we rest in utter confidence and self-distrust. It is an attitude which deflates pride, especially in our religious virtues and attainments, and exalts the sovereign grace of God, and his matchless gift on which we have no claim.

Confidence in the flesh, which the apostle mentions only to reject with horror, is but another way of expressing the innate tendency on the part of the religious person to obtain a standing before God and to secure, by one's own effort, approval and acceptance with him. In the case of the adversaries their confidence reposed in the rituals and rites of the cult as conferring by themselves the desired blessing of God. Here, then, the flesh may have some connection with the practice of circumcision (*cf.* Gal. 6:12–13; Eph. 2:11, 15); or it may be a contrast with 'in the

---

[1]For a discussion on 'The Holy Spirit in our Worship', see R. P. Martin, *The Worship of God. Some Theological, Pastoral and Practical Reflections* (Paternoster/Eerdmans, 1982), ch. 10.

spirit' as in Romans 2:28–29 (*cf.* note on 3:19). At all events this false confidence stands in direct opposition to the person and work of Christ. As Calvin points out, to place one's confidence, *i.e.* one's trust, in anything outside of Christ is to have *confidence in the flesh*; and this would subvert the gospel and endanger the soul. Therefore such confidence is to be rejected.[1]

B. PAUL'S AUTOBIOGRAPHY (3:4–14)

1. *His Jewish inheritance* (3:4–6)

This clear statement of the church's position *vis-à-vis* Judaism, and therefore the Jewish Christian teachers, paves the way for a full exposure of the life and experience of one who did at one time have 'confidence in the flesh'. Paul draws back the curtain and allows the Philippians to see what his past religious life was like so that they may be able to understand why he has warned them so plainly.

Up to verse 6 his past career is viewed from the standpoint of his former profession. The turning-point in this assessment comes at verse 7. The section, verses 4–6, needs to be studied with this point of view always in mind and it forms, in the words of Bonnard, 'one of the most remarkable personal confessions which antiquity has bequeathed to us'. The apostle seems to be at great pains to make clear his own position; and the reason for this will be the argument of the opponents that his teaching needed supplementing by the addition of certain ceremonies, notably circumcision. He provides a complete armoury against the arguments of their false doctrine by recounting his own experience under the law, his conversion to Christ, and his assessment of the results of his conversion in terms of what he lost and what he received.

4. *Anyone else* looks at the hypothetical debater, and challenges him to a duel of comparison. Is he as qualified as Paul

---

[1]For 'flesh' in Paul's teaching see Martin, *Reconciliation*, pp. 59–61.

was, as competent to judge the issue, as meticulous in his profession? To every advantage that such a man may claim, Paul retorts, *I have more*. Again, it is 'as a fool' (2 Cor. 11:16ff.; 12:11) that he speaks, deliberately putting himself back into the past, and reviewing it through pre-Christian eyes. In order, however, to make clear this right to speak, and for the Philippians' sakes to answer the insinuations of his opponents, he must list his credentials. The necessities of polemic force him to show himself an 'authentic Jew' (Benoit), in a way similar to 2 Corinthians 11:21ff. This he now proceeds to do.

5. There follows a descriptive list of his qualifications to speak as a true, full-blooded Jew. The seven advantages he enjoyed are in two categories, and they are retailed, as Bengel says quaintly, as though Paul were numbering them concisely and pointedly on the fingers of his hands. Four items in the catalogue were his possessions by involuntary heredity; the other three were his by personal choice and conviction.

Circumcised on the eighth day, lit. 'as to circumcision, eight days old', proves both his parents' conformity to the letter of the law (Lv. 12:3) and his true 'Jewishness'. He was no proselyte, circumcised in later life as some of his enemies might have been if they were adult converts to Jewish Christianity; nor was he an Ishmaelite who was circumcised after the thirteenth year of his life (Gn. 17:25; *cf.* Josephus, *Antiquities*, 1. 12, 2). The proudest claim is put first: he is a true-blooded Jew from the cradle, and nursed in the ancestral faith. Therefore he speaks with an authority which none can challenge, least of all the opponents whose main tenet in their expected approach to the Philippian church may have been the need of circumcision. Paul would counter this false notion by placing circumcision at the head of his list to show that he has the right to be heard on the true significance of the rite.

From correct observation of the Jewish national badge the apostle next reviews his favoured position as belonging to *the people of Israel*. Here *Israel* is the covenant name of the elect race, and Paul is proud to claim membership of it (*cf.* 2 Cor. 11:22; Rom. 11:1) as a 'full-blooded Jew' (Gnilka).

Within the national life of God's chosen people he claimed adherence to a special tribe, that *of Benjamin*. This tribe was regarded with particular esteem, in spite of its smallness ('little tribe of Benjamin', Ps. 68:27), and various reasons for its place of honour are suggested. Situated in the south it may have resisted the encroachments of paganism from the north (so Gnilka). It had the unique privilege of containing the holy city and the Temple within its confines. It remained loyal to the house of David after the disruption of the monarchy, and earlier, in the field of battle, it held the post of honour (Jdg. 5:14; Ho. 5:8). One suspects, however, that it was the fact that Israel's first king was drawn from its ranks (1 Sa. 9:1–2, 21; 10:1, 20–25) and that this king had the apostle's original Hebrew name which gave him special pride in his tribal association (so Beare).

A Hebrew of Hebrews carries the meaning as given in Moffatt's translation, 'the Hebrew son of Hebrew parents', and informs us that the language in which he was reared and taught was the ancestral mother-tongue of his race. Ability to speak the ancient languages (Hebrew and Aramaic) was a mark of faithfulness to the old culture, and commanded special attention, as we know from the scene in Acts 22:2 when Paul addressed the crowd in Aramaic. Jerome preserves a tradition that Paul's family fled to Tarsus in Cilicia (Acts 21:39; 22:3) from a town in Galilee when the Romans devastated Palestine. If there is substance in this tradition it would be a further claim to racial purity, but it seems likely that Jerome's tradition took its rise from this text.

The apostle now mentions the three privileges which he could boast of as his personal acquirement. In regard to his devotion to the law, the venerable Torah which the Jews prized so highly, he could own his membership of the strictest sect of his religion (Acts 26:5), the Pharisees (Gal. 1:14).[1]

6. His zeal as a Pharisee is shown in his self-confessed hatred of the Nazarenes, *i.e.* the early Christians, and his active persecution of their communities at Jerusalem and Damascus (see

[1]On this party as representing the most devoted and exacting element within the Jewish community, compare Josephus, *Antiquities*, 17.2,4, 18.1,3; *Jewish War*, 2.8, 14, and the discussion in J. Jeremias, *Jerusalem in the Time of Jesus* (ET, SCM, 1969), pp. 246–267.

Acts 22:3ff.; 26:10ff.; 1 Cor. 15:9; Gal. 1:13; 1 Tim. 1:13). Paul seems never to have been able to forget his persecuting activity, based on that misdirected *zeal* for God (Acts 22:3; *cf.* Rom. 10:2) and his cause, of which he speaks here. The memory of it continually haunts him; so much so that he uses the present participle of the verb, *diōkōn, persecuting,* as if the action were before his eyes at the time of writing. But he does know, too, the mercy of God in forgiveness and conversion (1 Tim. 1:12–13) which turned the arch-persecutor into the faithful apostle and fearless missionary of the one whom he had opposed in *persecuting the church* (Acts 9:4–5). The use of the word 'church' here shows that the term embraces not simply various local communities of Christians but rather the church of God ('of God' is read by some MSS) in the 'ecumenical' sense of the one body of Christ which, in the words of K. L. Schmidt, 'is truly present in its wholeness in every company of believers, however small'.[1]

Judged by the standard of legal righteousness he was, in his own eyes, *faultless, amemptos* (*cf.* the same word in 2:15). It is important to remember the standard by which he is measuring his past life. The carefully worded criterion is 'righteousness under the law' (RSV), and it is only by reference to the observance of this law that his verdict can be recorded as *faultless*.[2] Paul, as a Christian, never acquiesced in that judgment upon his past life as we know from Romans 7 and Galatians 2. Here he says nothing of the inner conflict and tension which his life under the law provoked because his viewpoint is completely different. This verse is only part of the story and must be supplemented and corrected by the true picture the apostle paints elsewhere.[3]

There is evidence that some rabbis held out the possibility of blamelessness through a strict observance of the law, provided the performance were punctilious and complete. Paul here claims to have qualified – by that standard.

[1]See *TDNT*, 3, p. 506.   [2]See Martin, *Reconciliation*, pp. 24–31, especially p. 26.

[3]This assumes that Romans 7 is an autobiographical transcript of Paul's own experience in the days before his conversion (so C. H. Dodd, *The Epistle of Paul to the Romans* [Hodder and Stoughton, 1932], pp. 107, 108). For another reading of Romans 7, see J. D. G. Dunn, 'Romans 7:14–25 in the Theology of Paul', *Theologische Zeitschrift*, 31, 1975, pp. 257–273.

2. His past renunciation, present aim and future hope (3:7–14)

7. The time has now come, in the sequence of the chapter, for the apostle to state clearly the reassessment of his spiritual life, which followed directly upon conversion. This is introduced by a strong asseveration: *But whatever was to my profit I now consider loss for the sake of Christ.* The last words supply the motive and reason for this dramatic revaluation. Because of all that Christ has become to him Paul is willing to collect all his former privileges, described in verses 5–6, to put them, as it were, in one parcel, and write that off as *loss.* He is not content simply to dismiss them and become indifferent to them. Rather, as Barth suggests, he rejects them with horror, and treats them as liabilities.

The contrast between *profit* and *loss* is a rabbinic one,[1] and underlies the teaching of Jesus in Matthew 16:26; Mark 8:36. The words of the Master paralleled in the Jewish tradition may very well have been in the apostle's mind as he saw their fulfilment in his past life.

The tense of *I now consider* is the Greek perfect, denoting an action in past time which is effective in the present. It refers to the choice of his conversion, on its human side, and reminds us that the transformation of Paul's life did not come about gradually and unconsciously. It came dramatically with abiding effects. This strong verb, *hēgēmai,* used in 2:6, witnesses to the conscious and personal decision which he made in response to the grace of God and the call of Christ. Beyond all doubt, the encounter of the Damascus road (Acts 9:6) is in view in this verse.[2]

8. The progression of the apostle's thought is marked by the strong particles of the original, *alla men oun ge kai* which is translated *what is more.* We are prepared then by this forceful introduction for an important announcement. Paul's range of thought is extended now to include not only the religious

---

[1] Strack-Billerbeck, i, p. 749; *cf. Aboth* 2:1.
[2] See Seyoon Kim, *The Origin of Paul's Gospel* (Eerdmans, 1982), pp. 56, 297–300.

advantages of the earlier verses, but *everything* which might conceivably be reckoned as meritorious and claimed as acceptable to God by the 'religious' person. A more complete indictment of 'religion' with its attempt to appear before God on the ground of its merit and privileges can hardly be imagined. Whatever may be regarded as a prop to support the person who hankers after something to boast about and is blind to the fact that he or she can live only by the grace of God, or as a virtue which he would call his own, is counted *loss* and *rubbish*.

The vigorous language and the widened scope of the apostle's confession support Heinzelmann's view that Paul has in mind here, not so much the decision of many years before at his conversion, but his ever present choice against a recurring temptation to rely on anything apart from Christ. So the tense passes from the perfect to the present. In the scales of his choice all the privileges he could claim as a Jew (vv. 5–7) and as a Christian (v. 8) were offset by inestimable gain. This is stated in terms of 'knowledge' (*cf.* v. 10) which is described in such a way as to leave the reader in no doubt about its uniqueness. *Knowing Christ Jesus my Lord* is not only superior to the privileges of Judaism and 'religion': it excels them to such a degree, and so far outstrips them, that it must be considered in a class apart.

The verse uses a noun 'knowledge', *gnōsis*, which Paul received as God's gift in the illumination of his conversion experience; the noun corresponds to the Hebrew *daᶜath* from the verb *yadaᶜ*, 'to know'. For example, it is used of God's knowledge of his people in election and grace (in Am. 3:2, of the nation; in Ex. 33:12, 17 and Je. 1:5, of an individual; *cf.* 2 Tim. 2:19), and their knowledge of him in love and obedience (see Je. 31:34; Ho. 6:3; 8:2). The Pauline expression 'to know Christ' is intimate (*my Lord*), and glows with the warmth of a direct relationship; it may therefore be taken as equivalent to 'fellowship with Christ' to which Paul was introduced on the day of his conversion (*cf.* 2 Cor. 4:6). This encounter with the living Christ set up a moral and spiritual union by faith which he expresses elsewhere by the celebrated phrase, 'in Christ' (*cf.* 2 Cor. 5:17; 12:2).

The intimate relationship with *Christ Jesus* into which Paul has been brought was not secured without a price. Answering to the divine revelation of the Lord there went the forfeiture of his 'gains' and surrender of his pride on the part of the apostle: *for whose sake I have lost all things*, translates *ezēmiōthēn* which is related to *zēmia*, *loss*, in the previous and present verses. The aorist tense looks back to a definite occasion when the transaction took place, and this is undoubtedly the great renunciation involved in his commitment to Christ on the way to Damascus.

For the third time Paul uses the same verb, *consider*, to declare his determined resolve to have done with his old life, which has passed away (see Gal. 6:14), and to revise his estimate of those things which formerly were the ground of his claim upon God. In the light of this new valuation, seen now through his enlightened eyes (Eph. 1:18) and with a mind renewed by the Spirit of God (1 Cor. 2:11–15; Eph. 4:23) these things are dismissed and rejected by the vulgar term, *rubbish*, AV/KJV 'dung'. It may be, however, that the KJV translation is too strong. *Skybala* can mean simply 'refuse' (RSV) or 'mere garbage' (GNB American ed.). The derivation is a choice between human waste product and the unwanted food which is consigned to the rubbish heap. The attempt to connect the latter with the mention of 'dogs' in verse 2 is rather fanciful, although the derivation of *skybalon* from *es kynas balein*, 'to throw to the dogs', is accepted by Moulton-Milligan. A word like 'muck' conveys to the modern reader something of the distaste and disgrace of the original term; and such an expression shows how completely the apostle has turned from his pre-converted ways. All 'confidence in the flesh' is contemptuously cast aside and abhorred as dirty muck (*cf.* Is. 64:6; Zc. 3:3–5). Such is God's estimate of all religious observance and practice which is not rooted in Christ and his atoning merit (Hawthorne).

The goal of Paul's revaluation is the supreme one of a personal possession. He loses all, to gain – Christ. Here, *that I may gain*, *kerdēsō*, pairs up with the 'gain', *kerdos*, of verse 7 as the words 'loss' and *have lost* also do. In what sense could Paul gain Christ? The answer lies probably with the thought of the personal appropriation of Christ by the believer; or possibly the thought is that of Paul's foundation which rests solely upon Christ. He is concerned to have him as his all-sufficient Saviour and the ground of his righteousness so that, in the day of judgment, he may have the vital possession (see 1:11), the justifying righteousness of Christ which comes in Christ himself (*cf.* 1:21, where 'to die' is *kerdos* for the apostle). The person and work of Christ are inseparably joined. To *gain* him is to have him as one's all-prevailing merit; and, in the classic words of Melanchthon, to know him in the intimacy of personal trust and surrender is to know his saving benefits.

Whatever the precise sense of these profound terms, Paul here speaks for all who bear the name of Christian, not for a select group, whether so-called 'mystics' (Dibelius) or martyrs (Lohmeyer). All need to renounce pride, and seek in Christ alone the source of their salvation.

9. The apostle's thought moves on to the future day of judgment with the longing he has to *be found in him*. Compare Galatians 2:17 where Lightfoot points out that the verb involves the idea of a surprise. The exact meaning of the phrase is explained by what follows; as Bonnard says, 'to be in Christ is nothing else than having the righteousness which comes from God'. The possession of this righteousness is the one essential for acquittal at the tribunal of God. Therefore Paul makes it clear, first, that such righteousness is in diametrical contrast to *a righteousness of my own, i.e.* it cannot be acquired by human effort on the basis of *the law*. Secondly, he stresses that it comes to the believer as the gift of God in Christ. *The righteousness that comes from God* is a description which looks back to Isaiah 54:17, *cf. Baruch* 5:2, 9, which reads, 'Put on the robe of the righteousness from God . . . with the mercy and righteousness that come from him' (RSV translation). He is the sole author of the saving righteousness imparted to sinful men. Thirdly, the medium through which the divine righteousness (or God's saving power, put forth on behalf of his people, as in Is. 46:13; 51:5) reaches us is *faith*. It is *through* faith, *dia pisteōs*, in Christ, and *by* faith, *epi tē pistei, i.e.* on the basis of human response to the offer of the gospel. The initiative is with God in his provision of a saving righteousness in Christ, and human faith is the grateful acknowledging of this provision and acceptance of it.[1]

10. The force of the grammatical construction translated *I want to know Christ* is open to a number of different interpretations. It may express purpose, 'in order that I may know him', parallel to 'that I may gain Christ' in verse 8; or it may point to the result, 'so that I may know him'; or there may be an extension of the ideas previously expressed (the explanatory use of the infinitive, *tou gnōnai*) with the meaning that God's righteousness received by faith makes it possible for the believer to know Christ and his saving benefits.[2]

This knowing Christ is another way of expressing the personal faith-union set up between the Christian and his Lord; and it is further explained in the words which follow, *and* having the sense of 'namely', 'that is'. *The power of his resurrection* is the power, *dynamis*, of Christ liberated by his victory over death, and at work in the life of the believer, raising him from the death of sin into the newness of life in Christ (see Rom. 6:4ff.; Eph. 1:19ff.; 2:5). *The fellowship of sharing in (koinōnia) his sufferings* describes the close affinity between the Lord's sufferings on the cross and the lot of the apostle who, in the life to which God called him, represented Christ so realistically that his apostolic sufferings were regarded as an extension of the 'dying of Jesus' borne in his mortal body (2 Cor. 4:10; *cf.* Rom. 8:36). There can hardly be any other meaning of these verses which so dramatically set forth the significance which Paul gives to his sufferings for Christ's sake. See further on *koinōnia*, in the Introduction, pp. 48–52.

Conformity to Christ's *death* is best explained in the light of Romans 8:29 and Philippians 3:21. It involves the teaching and experience of Romans 6, where the death and resurrection of

---

[1]For a bibliography of 'the righteous of God', see Martin, *Philippians* (NCB, 1976=1980), pp. 131–133; and J. Reumann, *Righteousness in the New Testament* (Fortress, 1982), especially pp. 62, 63 for pertinent comment on 3:9–11, but the preference for Collange's cumbrous translation is open to doubt.

[2]*Cf.* Collange and Hawthorne for some technical discussion of the grammar here.

Christ are representative acts in which his people share. His death for sin, and to sin, carried the implication that in him we likewise die to the dominion of the old nature and rise to newness of life. When he died at Calvary our death was involved; but its outworking requires the exhortation of Romans 6:11, which is another way of saying, 'Be conformed to his death'. Death, however, is the gateway to life. Paul dies to himself that he may live to God (Gal. 2:20). Self, represented by his past life as a Pharisee (see vv. 4–6), is dethroned – indeed, crucified (Gal. 5:24; 6:14) – that Christ might be enthroned as supreme Lord.[1]

11. Paul goes on, however, to make it clear that the completion of the work of grace awaits *the resurrection from the dead*. Here and now the Christian is risen with Christ, and is living in the power of his victorious life; but the believer still cherishes the prospect of a consummation when inner conflict (Gal. 5:16ff.) will be resolved in the perfection of the blessed state following the resurrection. This is the 'not yet' quality about the Christian life (Getty). The phrase is literally 'the resurrection from among corpses', *exanastasin* (here only in the New Testament) *tēn ek nekrōn*. Compare Luke 20:35 for a similar phrase. It is the resurrection of the righteous in both passages. It is probable that this reference is called forth by the existence of some heretical teaching, as at Corinth, which implied that the only resurrection hope of the believer had already been fulfilled in the experience of the new birth (1 Cor. 15:12; *cf.* 2 Tim. 2:18 and Polycarp's letter to the Philippians, 7:1).[2]

The apostle looks forward longingly to complete conformity to his Lord (3:21). He does not doubt he will be raised. The qualification *and so, somehow* (*ei pōs*, suggesting a clause in which the attainment of a purpose is not altogether within the subject's power; so Bruce) reflects the same uncertainty of his immediate future which was noted in 1:22–23, *i.e.* it relates to the immedi-

---

[1] Tannehill, *Dying and Rising with Christ*, has some fine writing on what he calls 'the power of conformation' based on this verse (pp. 104–112).

[2] See Martin, *The Spirit and the Congregation*, pp. 107–144.

ate prospect of his trial and its issue, which hangs in the balance at the time of writing. He would cherish the prospect of death as a decisive step nearer the resurrection, but acknowledges that it may be God's will for him to remain alive for the Philippians' sakes. There is no lack of certainty about his salvation and ultimate bliss. He knows that nothing can separate him from the love of God (Rom. 8:38–39): what is in doubt is the way he will go home to God, whether by martyrdom or not.

12. This verse marks the opening of a section in which Paul states the tension between his present attainment and his aspiration for the future. The key words are *obtained*, and *take hold* (especially the latter). In the passive voice, *katelēmphthēn* is rendered by an active in NIV: *Christ Jesus took hold of me*; it looks back to the time of his conversion. The aim of the apostle is set out in his desire to *take hold* of (*katalabō*), *i.e.* to make his own possession, the purpose for which the risen Christ appeared to him, and he frankly confesses that the goal of his endeavour has not yet been *taken hold* of. Hence his whole life is a pressing on to a future goal.[1]

The perfection he has in view needs careful definition. A backward glance at the preceding verse with its reference to the resurrection of the dead suggests that what he has in mind is that perfection which will be his only at the resurrection; and this state he obviously has not yet attained. The apostle denies, then, any sense of final perfection as a present experience, with his eye probably on a teaching which some Philippians were following. This doctrine claimed the fullness of perfection here and now, possibly on the mistaken belief that believers were 'already risen' to the fullness of their life in Christ in baptism.

By his allusion to the future resurrection he makes it clear that the work of sanctifying grace is progressive, that the believer lives within the tension of salvation begun now but not yet final, and that the *summum bonum* of Christian experience will be

---

[1] This verse has a lot to tell us about how Paul viewed conversion: see J. Dupont, 'The Conversion of Paul, and its influence on his understanding of salvation by faith', in *Apostolic History and the Gospel*, ch. 11.

reached only at the parousia or coming of Christ. Final perfection cannot be expected in this life and there will always be room for progress while the church is God's pilgrim people.

> Ah, but a man's reach should exceed his grasp,
> Or what's a heaven for?   (Browning)

But there is a relative perfection, appropriate to our state as redeemed and sanctified believers, which Paul himself knew and expected of his converts (*cf.* Eph. 4:13; Col. 1:28). See further the note on verse 15.

Meanwhile he continues his course. The verb *diōkō*, translated here and in verse 14 *press on*, is a hunting word meaning 'I pursue'; it is also used of foot-racing. It is a strong expression for active and earnest endeavour. It is correlative with *take hold* in a number of passages (Rom. 9:30; *cf.* Ex. 15:9; 2 *Clement* 18:2) in the sense of 'pursue and overtake', 'chase and capture'. This gives an excellent sense. The apostle presses forward in his Christian course in the full recognition that he is not yet perfect, but lives in confidence of ultimate salvation. If the attainment of perfection is denied, there is equally no quietism or indifferent acquiescence in his present experience. He is concerned to strain every nerve to pursue the ideal before him, and at last to capture the coveted prize (v. 14). See on the next verse.

13. The disclaimer, *Brothers, I do not consider myself yet to have taken hold*, is repeated from verse 12. Here again the object of the verb is either the full knowledge of Christ, of which a foretaste was given at his conversion, or the blessedness of the resurrection. The former is preferable in view of what follows. Notice the important addition of 'yet' made by the NIV, following the best texts. This addition is required by the context, although the MS evidence makes a choice between AV/KJV 'not', *ou*, and NIV *not yet*, *oupō*, difficult. There is no complacency which cuts the nerve of progress or stifles the hope of final perfection; and no sinful contentment with his own present position.

The apostle's resolute motto for life is contained in his confession. *But one thing I do* is literally the terse: 'but – one thing', *hen de*. He is evidently much moved as he dictates. His thought is agitated, his speech staccato, his words abrupt. The *one thing* is left undefined, and it is to be inferred from the words which follow. *Forgetting what is behind* is a glance at the apostle's past life, whether in regard to his Jewish prerogatives which are enumerated in verses 5–6, or in reference to his past experiences as a Christian, the successes and failures, triumphs and miseries which came to him as an apostle. In support of the first alternative is the awareness we have detected in verse 8 that the tendency to revert to 'confidence in the flesh' would, if he should yield to it, only impede his progress. This was precisely the fault of the Galatians who, under pressure of the Judaizers who would impose a yoke of bondage (Gal. 5:1) and expose them to the danger of returning to their former allegiance (Gal. 4:9), were being obstructed in their spiritual advance (Gal. 5:7). Paul overcame the temptation by a deliberate and continuous *forgetting, epilanthanomenos* (a present participle). 'To forget', in the biblical sense of the word, is not just simply to obliterate from the mind (if that is indeed possible). It is rather the opposite of 'remembering' (*anamnēsis*), which, as a biblical term, carries the important dynamic meaning of a recalling from the past into the present of an action which lies buried in history, in such a way that the result of the past action is made potently present. 1 Kings 17:18 illustrates this. The widow accuses Elijah of 'recalling' her sin from the past, and the potency of this 'recalling' is seen in the death of her son. Paul intends to forget his past in this sense. He will not regard it as having any bearing or influence upon his present spiritual outlook or conduct.

Matching this negative attitude is a positive concentration on the worthwhile exercise of *straining towards what is ahead*. It is the picture of a runner who strains every effort to press forward in the race.[1] The prospects of the finishing post and the prize of victory spur him on so that he 'may finish the race' (Acts 20:24). To do this he must 'run without swerving' (1 Cor. 9:26, Moffatt),

---

[1] For the word 'strain', *ekteinō* see V. C. Pfitzner, *Paul and the Agon Motif* (Brill, 1967), pp. 139–156.

and with the utmost effort. Paul clearly has in mind here the events of the last day, the resurrection, and the judgment which will also hold the distribution of rewards to the faithful believers (1 Cor. 3:14; 9:25; 2 Tim. 4:8).

14. The thought of the reward is now taken up at greater length. To gain *the prize* at the conclusion of his earthly race the apostle sets his eye on the *goal, skopon* (the cognate verb *skopein*, 'to watch', 'to look' is used in 2:4), and presses, *diōkō*, towards it (see on v. 12). He does not define what the coveted prize will be. *God has called me heavenwards* (lit. 'the call to "come up"', spoken to Paul)[1] does not denote its content but rather that God's call has come to him in order that he might enter for and attain the prize. That call was heard and answered at Paul's conversion, and was addressed to him by Christ Jesus. It is the same call which is addressed to believers in the mercy of God, summoning them out of their rebellion and sin into fellowship with himself in Christ on the ground of his reconciliation on the cross. Therefore it is a 'high' or 'upward' calling, leading us to God himself.

As Christ himself is the foundation of the divine summons to sinful men and women, and the one through whom it is addressed, so we may believe that he is *the prize* (Bruce). Bengel, however, interprets this expression as meaning the crown of life (*cf.* 1 Cor. 9:25; 2 Tim. 4:8; Jas. 1:12). The notion of merit is entirely excluded by the reminder that God's enabling call and persevering grace are required before the race can be completed. Our part is to remain 'worthy of his calling' (2 Thes. 1:11), and to press on to the finishing of our course with patience and courage, looking to Jesus (Heb. 12:1–2).

C. PAUL'S CALL FOR UNITY IN CONVICTION AND CONDUCT
(3:15–17)

15. It is evident from this verse that the foregoing discussion

---

[1]See *ad loc.* Collange, Martin, Hawthorne for the background in the Olympic Games.

on Christian perfection was set against a background of controversy. Apparently, in the Philippian church, there were
those who tended to *think differently*, *i.e.* to adopt a different
viewpoint from that given in Paul's teaching and to act upon it.
The use of the verb *phronein* shows that it was more than an
intellectual difference; it betrayed a different outlook and
affected the conduct of those whom Paul has in mind. Clearly
there were some who were teaching that it was possible to be
'perfect' in a final sense here and now. The apostle answers
this in a twofold way. First, he insists on a true evaluation of
perfection in terms of a maturity which ever seeks a fuller
maturity. This is the meaning of the admission, *all of us who are
mature*, *i.e.* 'spiritually mature' (GNB), where the word used is
teleioi which can signify 'complete, fully developed according to
a present standard', as in 1 Corinthians 14:20 and Hebrews
5:14. There is no contradiction of verse 12; and no hint that he
is using the term *mature* ironically as Lightfoot suggests. He is
opposing a relative and progressive 'perfection' which he
expects of every Christian to the impossible claim of final perfection which must ever be future while we are still on earth.
There may have been a group in the Philippian church who
professed a spiritual attainment superior to that of the rest of
their fellow-believers whom they may have despised, in much
the same way as the later gnostics looked down upon those
who could never attain the rank of the *teleioi*. Paul would deny
this exclusive claim.

The second counterblast to the claim of false perfection is the
suggestion that if any are disposed to think differently *that too*
(*i.e.* Paul's statement of true perfection and not some idea he
judged to be alien to his teaching) *God will make clear to you*. So
confident is he that the truth has been stated, that he invokes
the aid of God to illuminate the minds and correct the
behaviour of those who do not share his conviction (*cf.* Gal.
5:10).

There is a point of contact between the situation described
here and the state of the Corinthian church. The same spirit of
pride based on wrong-headed claims to a false understanding
of the resurrection prevailed in the church at Corinth, and

showed itself in a kindred symptom, *viz.* dissension and quarrelsomeness among the church members.[1]

16. This verse, which reads more literally, 'Only as far as we have attained, by the same let us walk', is a tacit and tactful way of calling the readers to an acceptance of the truth as Paul has expounded it earlier in the chapter. The apostle is confident that a desire to know the truth in full measure will be rewarded by God's revelation (v. 15). Meanwhile, he says, until you have fuller light, be content to be open-minded and teachable, and guide your life by the light you have received. Later church history is ample proof of the discord and bad feeling which the various interpretations of the doctrine of sanctification and a faulty understanding of Christian living have caused. The apostle's moderate and eirenical words, if they had been remembered, would have prevented such unhappy scenes.

17. To any who might object that the standard of conduct was not clear, Paul replies with words which set before his readers a living pattern of behaviour by which they may shape their lives. This is his own example, and the example of those whose lives were based on his. For Christianity the pattern of ethical teaching is embodied not in a written code of precepts and maxims covering every possible contingency of life, but in a life – pre-eminently the life of the Lord Jesus, and secondarily in the lives of his earliest and closest followers. This is the New Testament counterpart to the Hebrew term *halākāh*, *i.e.* practical conduct (lit. 'walking', as in Ps. 1:1) as distinct from mental activity. So the apostle uses the Greek verbs *stoichein*, *peripatein*, which are the literal rendering of the Hebrew. For us today, access to that pattern is possible through the opened Bible in which we read of the life which was the light of the world, and the renewing Spirit (2 Cor. 3:6) who enables us to apply gospel teaching to our modern situations. But the lives of the many outstanding men and women of God, in whom his grace has shone, must also be considered.

[1] For details, see Martin, *The Spirit and the Congregation*.

Paul's claim to be an example to others, *join . . . in following my example . . . according to the pattern we gave you*, may seem to be egotistical and vain, but 1 Corinthians 11:1 is a qualifying factor: 'Follow my example, as I follow the example of Christ,' or 'as I belong to Christ'. The *pattern*, *typos*, of the apostle and his associates (Timothy, Epaphroditus; *cf.* 1 Thes. 1:6; 2 Thes. 3:7, 9), whose lives the Philippians are closely to *take note of*, *skopeite* (*cf.* v. 14 and 2:4), is here not a vague ethical ideal. It refers to the teaching of the preceding verses. Like the apostle, they must learn to renounce all 'man-made' righteousness, and place themselves under the judgment of the cross, with its summons to a death to sin and a life in fellowship with God (v. 10). Like him also, they must throw off complacency and press forward in their Christian course (vv. 12, 14). So the call is less one of imitation and more of recognizing Paul's apostolic authority.[1]

D. SECTARIAN TEACHERS TO BE SHUNNED (3:18–19)

18–19. The practical conduct of Paul and his fellow-workers is the Philippians' goal and aim. But let them turn away from another example set by *many* professing Christians whose lives are a disgrace to the name they claim to bear, and a source of pain to the apostle himself. The persons here referred to are evidently professed believers, as Kennedy has convincingly demonstrated,[2] but whether they are Jewish or Gentile it is hard to decide.

If they were Jewish Christians and are, therefore, the same group as Paul describes in 3:2ff., a number of allusions are explained. Their enmity to *the cross of Christ* is shown by their adherence to the law as an agent of salvation, thus subverting the necessity for and saving significance of the sacrifice of Cal-

---

[1] W. Michaelis, *TDNT*, 4, pp. 667 ff.

[2] Kennedy, p. 461. He cites the following points: (1) the verb *live* (v. 18) is evidently used of Christians (*cf.* v. 17); (2) the apostle's tears would have no meaning unless the reference is to Christians, *cf.* Acts 20:31. But he does use similar emotional language of his yearning over his unbelieving compatriots in Romans 9:1–3; 10:1. (3) The description *enemies* is a mere platitude if the reference is to the heathen.

vary as the only means of redemption (*cf.* Gal. 2:21, RSV). Their *destiny is destruction*, which means that, cutting themselves off from the only hope of salvation in Christ alone (Gal. 5:4), they have no prospect except the doom which awaits unsaved humanity (*e.g.* Rom. 9:22). *Their god is their stomach* will then be a reference to their distinctions between clean and unclean foods, a characteristic trait of Jewish Christianity (see Acts 15; Rom. 14; 16:18; 1 Cor. 8–10; Col. 2:16). Another feature of the Jewish Christians' creed was circumcision (*cf.* 3:2, 5) and the apostle may be making a caustic allusion to this in the phrase, *their glory is in their shame*. *Glory* here is almost the equivalent of 'God', as in Psalm 106:20; and the Hebrew word for *shame, bōsheth*, is used in the Old Testament as a devastating caricature of the false gods, *ba*ᶜ*al, b*ᵉᶜ*ālim* which the Jews idolatrously worshipped (see, for example, Je. 11:13). If Paul has trust in circumcision in mind, the *shame* will be that of the nakedness of the human body which was required for the rite to be performed (*cf.* Gn. 2:25; 3:7, 10–11; Ezk. 16:8; Rev. 3:18). Nakedness and shame are placed side by side in parallelism in Micah 1:11 and Nahum 3:5. Their mind, *phronountes*, is centred upon *earthly things* because their confidence is built upon prescriptions and rituals which are obsolete with the coming of Christ and the adequacy of his gospel to meet the need of sinful people.

On the other hand, it is better to see these verses as describing Paul's opponents in 2 Corinthians 10–13, *i.e.* Jewish Christian gnosticizing teachers, and to pin-point their false ideas as a relaxation of the moral law. They had succumbed to a tendency known as antinomianism, *i.e.* a throwing off of the moral code and decent behaviour on the mistaken ground that the body was an irrelevance once the mind had been illumined and the soul redeemed. Hence moral restraints could be ignored, and no carnal sin could stain the pure soul. Opposing this false teaching Romans 6:1ff. shows the impossibility of using the doctrine of grace as a ground of licence; 1 Corinthians 6:9ff. teaches the sacredness of the body as the Spirit's shrine; 1 Corinthians 8 and the epistle to the Colossians state the corrective of a tendency to rely upon 'knowledge' as the all-important factor in Christian experience. But these references also make it plain that, in his churches, Paul had to combat erroneous teaching and sub-Christian practices which were destructive alike of his doctrine of grace and his insistence upon the highest morality.

If such false ideas are here condemned it is easy to fit in the references to *the enemies of the cross . . . their god is their stomach* (*koilia*, used of sexual organs as in 1 Cor. 6:13, Bruce) (*i.e.* their unbridled appetite and lusts), *their glory is in their shame* (*i.e.* immoral practices), *their mind is on earthly things* (*i.e.* their sensual pursuits). If such persons, cherishing a fond belief in their 'freedom' to do as they pleased, and playing fast and loose with morality (as at Corinth) are here in view, the stern words of Paul are much to the point. Michael remarks that such people can hardly have infiltrated into the ranks of the Philippian church, and he uses this point to support a partition theory which takes chapter 3 as separate from the rest of the letter. (See the Introduction, pp. 38–40.) But the data of 2 Corinthians 10–13 show that such an invasion had indeed taken place at Corinth (2 Cor. 11:3–4, 13–15); and the danger was a real prospect at Philippi. As with 3:1ff. Paul would warn the Philippians in advance of what they are likely to encounter (*cf.* Acts 20:29–30). *As I have often told you before* confirms this, and points to the identification with the schismatic teachers of Jewish origin (*cf.* 2 Cor. 11:22) and gnosticizing and antinomian tendency (*cf.* 2 Cor. 10:3–5; 12:21). See Collange and Hawthorne for other possibilities.

E. THE CHRISTIAN'S TRUE INHERITANCE (3:20–21)

20. The two previous verses were an aside, prompted by the use of the verb 'live' in verse 17. The true 'life' of the believer recalled to the apostle's mind the 'life' of the enemies of the gospel; and in the characterization of verses 18–19 he has exposed them in clear terms.

Now the same association of thought opens up a new contrast. The people who 'mind . . . earthly things' (v. 19) are set in direct contrast with the Christian whose *citizenship is in heaven*. It is *our* (placed first for emphasis) *citizenship* which is above, and not that of the enemy who has no part or lot in the true inheritance. *But, gar* (which is notoriously difficult to translate), will then express the contrast, 'however, to be sure'.

Citizenship, politeuma, may be rendered 'commonwealth' (RSV), 'behaviour' (*cf.* 1:27), or 'colony of heaven' (Moffatt). Dibelius paraphrases, 'We have our home in heaven, and here on earth we are a colony of heaven's citizens.' E. Stauffer, moreover, has shown that the only satisfactory sense of Paul's words here must be a translation of *politeuma* as a 'capital or native city, which keeps the citizens on its registers'.[1] The background of the word, in this context, is the situation of the readers who lived in a city which was a Roman military colony directly related to the capital city of Rome. (See the Introduction, pp. 17–20, and note on 1:27.)

The apostle here indicates the double allegiance of the Philippian Christians. As Roman subjects they are citizens of the far distant, capital city of Rome, where the emperor has his residence. As servants of 'another king, one called Jesus' (Acts 17:7), they are citizens of that capital city, where the King of kings has his domicile, and whose advent to establish his reign on this earth and to rescue his people (1 Thes. 1:10) is awaited. Here on earth, meanwhile, they are resident aliens who dwell temporarily in a foreign country, but have their citizenship elsewhere (*cf.* Heb. 11:13; Jas. 1:1; 1 Pet. 1:1; 2:11).[2]

From there, ex hou, can refer only to *politeuma,* and not to *ouranois, heaven* as the NIV might imply. From our capital city which is actually (Greek *hyparchei*) situated in the heavens we expect *a Saviour,* whose promised advent will bring the final deliverance from all the trials and persecutions of a hostile and alien world. *Saviour* is a very infrequent term when used as a title of the Lord Jesus in the Pauline writings. It is found only in Ephesians 5:23; 2 Timothy 1:10 and Titus 1:4; 2:13; 3:6. V. Taylor explains this neglect of the term in early Christian literature as due to the popular use of the designation in Greek religion

[1]Stauffer, *New Testament Theology,* pp. 296–297. But there is also a Jewish element in Paul's designation of the church. It is the community of Israel, as it is the 'true circumcision' (3:3, RSV), set in an alien world (Gnilka).

[2]We may compare with this the early Christian application of the teaching underlying Paul's term in the *Epistle to Diognetus* 5.

where the gods were hailed as 'saviours', and in Caesar worship which gave this honorific title to the emperor.[1] Christians would be reluctant to claim a term for their Lord which was so applied in current religious speech.

The use of the term here may be justified on the ground that Paul has employed an imagery in which the contrast with the Roman emperor was inevitable. Therefore, he opposes the true emperor, *the Lord Jesus Christ*, against the head of imperial Rome. *Saviour, sōtēr*, was a title of the Roman emperors since 48 BC when a decree of the people of Ephesus declared Julius Caesar to be the 'universal saviour of mankind'; thereafter it became a common title for the ruling Caesar.

Paul uses the word here in a descriptive sense. The attitude of the Christian, especially when undergoing trials such as the Philippians were experiencing (1:27-30; 2:15), is one of expectation which is centred upon the coming of Christ as Saviour (there is no definite article with the Greek *sōtēr*), *i.e.* in his capacity as vindicator of his people and as their deliverer from their oppressors. The picture, then, goes back to the Old Testament which often depicts God's coming to the aid of his afflicted people (*e.g.* Is. 35:4); but there is no evidence that here the adversaries persecuting the Philippian church were the Roman authorities, as Lohmeyer states. The contrast between the two emperors, Caesar and Christ, is a general one, possibly called forth from the peculiar civic situation of the Philippian Christians who lived in a Roman colony.

We eagerly await, apekdechometha, for his appearing, says Paul, using a verb which is usually employed of the hope which is set upon many things in the future (*cf.* Rom. 8:19, 23; 1 Cor. 1:7; Gal. 5:5). An exact parallel is Hebrews 9:28 which uses the same verb. The expected salvation, whether in the sense of our final redemption or complete deliverance from the hand of the persecutors of the church, is contrasted with the 'destruction', which is the fate of the persons referred to in verses 18-19.

---

[1] V. Taylor, *The Names of Jesus* (Macmillan, 1953), p. 109.

21. The purpose of the Lord's advent is explained further and, again, this verse looks back to a preceding mention of those whose sub-Christian view of the body is expressed in the words 'whose glory is in their shame, who mind earthly things' (AV). (Compare Col. 3:5 which exposes and trounces the sins of the body and uses a similar phrase, 'upon the earth'; and 2 Cor. 5:1.) This connection is preferable to Michael's view that it was the bodily suffering of both apostle and church which prompted the thought that the returning Lord will transform the believers' bodies.

Such a change as the apostle describes involves the complete transformation of our *lowly bodies*: 'vile' (AK/KJV) is too strong a translation for *tēs tapeinōseōs*. Literally the noun *tapeinōsis* means 'low estate', 'humiliation'; *cf.* 2:8, where the cognate verb is 'he humbled himself', and Luke 1:48. Ours is a lowly body because it belongs to the state of humiliation caused through sin. Its characteristics are frailty (*cf.* Gn. 3:19; Ps. 103:14) and weakness as the agency which sin finds it so easy to command and use (Rom. 7:14ff.). But the body itself as God's creation is good (1 Cor. 6:13ff.). There is no disparagement of the human body as inherently evil, as in stoic and gnostic thought.

'Our lowly body' will one day give place to a new 'spiritual' body. 1 Corinthians 15:42ff. describes also the transformation of the departed believers.[1] This present verse, together with 1 Thessalonians 4:15–17, has the church living on earth at the time of the Lord's return mainly in view. But the final result will be the same for both groups: the dead will be raised with glorified spiritual bodies; the living will be transformed. 'We will all (*i.e.* whether dead or alive) be changed' (1 Cor. 15:51).

'So shall we bear the image of the heavenly (one)', Christ in his glory (1 Cor. 15:49). This is the prospect held out by the words *like his glorious body*, *i.e.* the body which he possesses in his glorified and exalted state in contrast with the body he received at his incarnation (2:7–8; *cf.* Heb. 10:5f.). The 'body of his glory' is the prototype of the believer's spiritual body, and

---

[1]See Martin, *The Spirit and the Congregation*, pp. 134–142 for these and other verses given below in the text.

we shall be made like it, *symmorphon* (*cf. morphē*, 'form', in 2:6) by his transforming power; and so glorified together (Rom. 8:17; *cf.* Jn. 17:24). The likeness will not be external resemblance only, but we may say, in view of the use of the root *symmorphos* in 3:10, translated 'becoming like', that the point of connection will be a sharing in the nature of that exalted body, a partaking of its life and inherent qualities as truly and fully 'alive unto God' (see Rom. 6:10), a complete likeness to Christ (Rom. 8:29; 1 Jn. 3:2). With Michaelis we take *body, sōma*, to signify, not only the outward form, but 'the whole person'. The 'end-product' of God's redeeming activity, which is continuous throughout our Christian experience (2 Cor. 3:18) will then have been achieved: Christ will have taken shape (*morphē*) in us (*cf.* Gal. 4:19). The links, in both word association and ideas, with 2:6–11 should be observed (Martin, Hawthorne who speaks of these two verses (20–21) as 'one of the earliest hymns of the church').

The process of transformation is accomplished *by the power that enables him to bring everything under his control. Power, energeia*, represents energy in effective action (*cf.* Eph. 3:7) of which the resurrection of Christ is the supreme demonstration (Eph. 1:19–20). Here, however, Christ himself is the author of this mighty activity (as in Col. 1:29), and Paul is making it clear that the power required to change the bodies of believers is adequately provided for in the greater assurance that he is able to subject not only the intractable elements in the believer's make-up, but *everything*, the entire universe, *under his control*. The thought corresponds closely with that in 2:10–11 where every domain is brought into subjugation, and the cosmic confession is 'Jesus Christ is Lord' (so Michaelis, Hawthorne, Bruce). The reference to 'subjugation' is taken from Psalm 8:6, and its use here and in 1 Corinthians 15:27–28 and Hebrews 2:5–9 should be compared.[1]

[1]See Martin, *The Spirit and the Congregation*, pp. 112–114; A. T. Lincoln, *Paradise Now and Not Yet*, SNTSMS 43, (Cambridge University Press, 1981), pp. 87–109.

VIII. ENCOURAGEMENTS, APPRECIATIONS, GREETINGS (4:1-23)

A. ENCOURAGEMENTS TO STEADFASTNESS AND UNITY: APPRECIATION OF SERVICE (4:1-3)

1. The exhortation to *stand firm in the Lord* is to be taken as rounding off the previous section of the letter. Lohmeyer, however, unlike most commentators, regards this verse as a solemn and formal introduction to what follows. The apostle speaks warmly of his friends at Philippi in a language of endearing terms which are almost unique in his letters. The nearest parallel is in the Thessalonian correspondence.

Whom I . . . long for, epipothētoi, recalls 1:8, and expresses his ardent desire to see them again. *My joy and crown* are words of endearment reminiscent of Paul's tribute to the church at Thessalonica (1 Thes. 2:19-20; 3:9). The Greek word for *crown, stephanos,* besides the figurative meaning which expresses tender love, was commonly used to denote the festive garland, worn as a sign of gladness, or the wreath awarded to the victor at the athletic contest (*cf.* 1 Cor. 9:25). If the metaphor is to be applied here, it means that the Philippian Christians would be regarded as his 'reward', the seal of his apostleship (1 Cor. 9:2), and the proof that his labour had not been in vain in the Lord (1 Cor. 15:58; *cf.* Phil. 2:16). They would be his *crown* at the final day (*cf.* Pr. 12:4, 17:6 for this meaning of *stephanos* in LXX). Hebrews 13:17 contains the same idea that, at the last day, the triumph of grace will be seen in the perseverence of the saints to the inexpressible joy of their spiritual mentors. Therefore, the Philippians are encouraged to *stand firm* in union with *the Lord,* in spite of the fears and attacks which assail them from without and the encroachment of false doctrine into their church life.

2-3. Much fruitless effort has been expended in tracking a cryptic meaning in the names in these verses. *Euodia* and *Syntyche* are the names of women, presumably within the church fellowship, who had quarrelled; and it is natural to take the phrase *these women* in verse 3 as a reference to them. We know, then, that Paul looked upon them as his co-workers in some enterprise of the gospel.[1] Possibly they assisted him with material help as Lydia had done some years before (Acts 16:15, 40). They were evidently well known to the apostle who regrets their disagreement and urges them here *to agree with each other in the Lord*, *i.e.* as Christians should. *To agree* translates, *to auto phronein*, 'to have the same mind' is a phrase which uses Paul's favourite verb, *phronein* (see note on 1:7). The common 'mind' they are to share, in reconciliation and mutual love, is one which sets the good of the church above personal interest, and finds its inspiration in the lowliness of the incarnate Lord and the standard he expects of his people (2:3, 5). The reason for their quarrel is not given but it is clear from the wording that it was more than a personal disagreement (Bruce); their quarrel had ecclesiastical repercussions (Getty adds a pastoral comment: 'A continuing antagonism can only weaken the church and scandalize those who look for role models among their leadership').

Paul wishes to enlist the good offices of another Philippian believer in the task of reconciling the offended persons. He is designated rather curiously as *loyal yoke-fellow* which may be either a descriptive tribute to a Christian whose identity is concealed from us; or the two words may be taken together as a proper name: 'Syzygus (comrade), truly so called' (see NIV marg.). Lohmeyer, adopting the former alternative, calls him 'a brother in suffering' who was sharing Paul's imprisonment for the faith, although it is hard to see how he could help the women at a distance, and 2:20 is against this view. If we assume that the Greek *gnēsie syzyge* is to be translated as a proper name, the pun will find a parallel in the case of Onesimus in the letter to Philemon (*cf.* Phm. v. 11 for the play on the name which means 'useful, profitable'). In the case of 'Syzygus' Paul is playfully reminding him to be true to his name, and to be a real 'yoke-fellow', in assisting in the coming

[1]See W. D. Thomas, 'The Place of Women in the Church at Philippi', *ExpT*, 83, 1971–72, pp. 117–120.

together of the estranged women. If there is no pun, and the title hides the real name of another Christian, we have no means of knowing who it was, though Bruce nominates Luke in view of his attachment to the Philippian congregation (in Acts 16:12–40; Introduction, p. 20), and Timothy is called 'loyal' in 2:20 (Collange). Hawthorne opts for a veiled reference to the entire Philippian church – an unlikely, because complicated, solution to a riddle.

Clement is again the name of a Philippian Christian otherwise unknown. The attempt to equate him with Clement of Rome, the author of a letter to the Corinthians, is an exercise in the realm of conjecture (*cf.* Lightfoot's note on this). The name was a common one in the first century and would be familiar in a Roman colony like Philippi; so there is no clue to exact identification. Other nameless helpers are given honourable mention as *my fellow-workers* (as Epaphroditus was, 2:25). But, unnamed and unknown to us as they are, their names find a place in God's record, *the book of life*, wherein the names of the faithful, as the elect people of God in both covenant ages, are written (*cf.* Ex. 32:32; Ps. 69:28; 139:16; Lk. 10:20; and five or six times in Revelation, as well as in inter-testamental and rabbinical literature). Christian service may pass unnoticed on earth; the important thing is that God takes note, and will praise at the last (1 Cor. 4:5).

B. ENCOURAGEMENTS TO PRAYER AND NOBLE-MINDEDNESS (4:4–9)

4. Turning from the personal address of verses 2 and 3, the apostle confronts the whole church with a stirring call to *rejoice in the Lord* (see note on 3:1), followed by instruction in the practice of Christian virtues (vv. 5–9).

The appeal to constant rejoicing (*cf.* 1 Thes. 5:16) is no empty phrase. To a company of Christ's people, who were in doubt and fear (1:28) and set in the midst of a hostile world (2:15), this assurance rings out like a clarion call, and is repeated so that its message may not be misunderstood. Paul has the supreme qualification to issue the call, for he himself is engrossed in 'the same struggle' (1:30) as that which the Philippians are facing;

and, as they remember, his first visit (Acts 16:19–24) were the occasion of an impressive victory of faith and joy over despair (Acts 16:25). *In the Lord* is the governing factor in the exhortation. It is the Philippians' faith *in the Lord* which makes rejoicing in the throes of opposition a glorious possibility, as Bonnard finely comments: 'The Pauline appeals to joy are never simply encouragements; they throw back the distressed churches on their Lord; they are, above all, appeals to faith.'

5. The appeal to *gentleness, to epieikes* (RSV, 'forbearance'), is defined by the following words *to all*. This implies that the apostle has the church's relations with the outside world in mind rather than the Christian fellowship in its mutual relationships. *Epieikeia*, which is the noun corresponding to the adjective in the text, is an ethical term used again by Paul in 2 Corinthians 10:1. The LXX of Psalm 85 (86):5 uses the adjective to translate 'ready to forgive'; L. H. Marshall gives a full description of its meaning as 'fairmindedness, the attitude of a man who is charitable towards men's faults and merciful in his judgment of their failings because he takes their whole situation into his reckoning'.[1] Perhaps 'graciousness' is the best English equivalent; and, in the context here, it is to be the spirit of willingness to yield under trial which will show itself in a refusal to retaliate when attacked. It may have seemed an impossible ideal to the Philippians, but the preceding verse is a reminder that such a quality 'is the outshining of joy in the Lord', as Michaelis puts it.

The call to a gracious disposition made possible by God's grace is buttressed by a solemn warning of the Lord's nearness, *The Lord is near*. This is either a quotation from Psalm 145 (144 [LXX]):18 or a variation of the early Christian watchword and invocation of the Lord's coming, *Marana tha*, 'our Lord, come!' (1 Cor. 16:22; *cf.* Rev. 22:20). Michaelis, Caird, Bruce and Getty suggest the first alternative with the meaining of 'the nearness experienced in fellowship with the Lord'; Psalm 118 (119):151 in

---

[1] Marshall, *The Challenge of NT Ethics*, pp. 305–308; *cf.* Barclay, *New Testament Words*, pp. 38, 39.

LXX supports this. But the eschatological sense of the Lord's coming to vindicate his oppressed people (see note on 3:20) requires the second meaning (*cf.* 2 Thes. 1:7ff.). This meaning is supported by *Didache* 10:6 which proves that the Aramaic word is to be taken as an invocation and not as a statement as in some translations.[1] Compare also the wording of *Barnabas*, 21:3, 'The day is at hand when all things shall perish with the evil one; the Lord and his reward are at hand.' Both 'tenses' of the Lord's presence may be in view (Hawthorne).

6. The apostle's teaching on prayer in the present passage is one to which Christian people have turned for guidance and from which they have received encouragement and blessing, in every age. Remembering that the Philippians were encompassed by foes and had tended to become daunted (1:28; 3:1; 4:1), these words must have brought great comfort and hope. *Do not be anxious* is a negative command based on the idea that anxiety (*merimna*) betrays a lack of trust in God's care and is a species of 'unconscious blasphemy' against him (so Oswald Chambers); see Matthew 6:25–34; Luke 12:22 where the same verb is used. The continuation of the verse will then be 'a practical commentary' on the Lord's words, as Dibelius suggests.

The apostle can lay down this instruction as a command (*merimnate* is imperative) because he goes on: *but (alla) in everything, by prayer and petition*. The possibility and reality of *prayer* give the rationale of the first words of the sentence which, by themselves, seem so impossible to obey. We may be freed from all fretful care and feverish anxiety because we may refer all our distresses and problems to God in prayer. Thus Bengel's comment is so apt and true: anxiety and prayer (*curare et orare*) are more opposed to each other than fire and water.

Four terms are used in the vocabulary of the soul's inner life. *Prayer, proseuchē,* and *petition, deēsis,* are frequently found together in the apostle's writing and are distinguishable in two ways, according to G. Abbott-Smith's *Lexicon*. He says that

[1]See Martin, *The Worship of God*, pp. 148 f., 195–197.

proseuchē is used of prayer in general, while *deēsis* gives prominence to the sense of need. On the other hand, *deēsis* is used as well of requests from man to man, while *proseuchē* is limited to prayer to God. *Requests, aitēmata*, is a word which specifies the content of prayer as the formulating of definite and precise petitions (*cf.* Lk. 23:24; 1 Jn. 5:15). Prayer is thus saved from becoming a sentimental 'mooning before the Lord', to quote Oswald Chambers again; it can express itself in direct and specific *requests* (*e.g.* Lk. 11:5, 9–10). *Thanksgiving, eucharistia*, is an important accompaniment of true prayer. The recalling of God's goodness and mercy will save us from the many pitfalls which await the ungrateful soul, *e.g.* over-concern with our immediate problems, forgetfulness of God's gracious dealings with us in the past, disregard of the needs of others who are less fortunate than we are.

7. To careworn hearts the first effect of believing prayer is the enjoyment of God's *peace* which he has promised to all who are harassed and turn to him in trust (Is. 26:3). The genitive *of God* denotes origin (*cf.* 4:9b). It is the peace which he gives, and gives by virtue of his kingship. *Peace, eirēnē*, is in the Old Testament a kingly blessing following directly upon the acknowledgment of God's reign and the submission of all his foes (*shalom; cf.* Is. 32:17). In New Testament terms we can only know his peace as we first receive his grace in reconciliation (see note on 1:2).[1] *The peace of God* follows directly from peace with God through our Lord Jesus Christ (Rom. 5:1) who made that peace by the blood of his cross (Col. 1:20).

The descriptive phrase, *which transcends all understanding*, may signify 'achieving more than our clever forethought and ingenious plans can accomplish'; or 'transcending every human thought (*nous*), surpassing all our dreams' (*cf.* Moffatt), and therefore beyond the range of our comprehension (Eph. 3:20). The verb *transcends, hyperechousa*, is allied to the noun translated 'surpassing greatness' or 'excellency' in 3:8; and in both cases the meaning of absolute uniqueness, not relative

---

[1] In particular, see Martin, *Reconciliation*, pp. 139, 145–154 on Rom. 5:1 ff.

superiority, seems preferable. Hence the second translation is the correct one (Beare).

Paul uses a military metaphor in describing the activity of God's *peace*, which is almost personified. *Will guard, phrourēsei*, is better expressed in the military language of 'will keep guard over' (*cf.* 2 Cor. 11:32 for the verb in this sense). The Philippians, living in a garrison town, would be familiar with the sight of the Roman sentry, maintaining his watch. Likewise, comments the apostle, God's peace will garrison and protect *your hearts and your minds*. Bunyan's use of this picture in the appointment and patrol of Mr. God's-Peace in the town of Mansoul should be read in conjunction with this verse. 'Nothing was to be found but harmony, happiness, joy and health' so long as Mr. God's-Peace maintained his office. But when Prince Emmanuel was grieved away from the town, he laid down his commission and departed also. It is a salutary reminder that we enjoy God's gift only *in Christ Jesus*, *i.e.* by our obedience to him and submission to his authority. Paul amplifies this practical aspect in Colossians 3:15 where the peace of Christ is to 'rule', *i.e.* arbitrate, in the Christian heart, settling all doubtful issues and keeping the believer in constant dependence upon his Lord (GNB: 'Peace . . . [will] guide you in the decisions you make').

8. *Finally, to loipon* (*cf.* 3:1) may be taken as little more than 'and so', although it may have a logical connection with the foregoing verses and be translated: 'it follows then, in this connection'.[1] On the second view, the celebrated list of ethical terms, which *finally* introduces, will continue the thought of the peace of God in verses 8–9. This gives a good sense to the apostle's admonition. If inner tranquility is to be enjoyed continually and its influence shed abroad certain steps must be taken. The present verse is governed by the verb *think, logizesthe*, which means more than 'keep in mind' (Moffatt). It is rather 'take into account (*logos*), reflect upon and then allow these things to shape your conduct'. The following verse is a

---

[1]For the various connotations of *to loipon* see C. F. D. Moule, *An Idiom-Book of New Testament Greek* (Cambridge University Press, 1953), pp. 161, 162.

continuation of Paul's message with a call to explicit action: 'put it into practice'.

The use of ethical lists was a feature of stoic religion, and lists of vices and virtues are also found in the book of Wisdom and in Philo. It is, however, more important to note that all the terms used here, except the word translated *admirable*, are found in the LXX (full references are given in Lohmeyer). While it is true that, according to Dibelius, these ethical expressions are 'terms of popular moral philosophy' current in Paul's day, the LXX influence ought to be reckoned with as a strong factor guiding the apostle's thought.

The following words call for comment.[1] *Noble, semna*, may also be rendered 'honourable' (RSV) or 'worthy of honour'; or possibly, 'dignified, elevated'. *Lovely, prosphilē*, is found only here in the New Testament and, when used of things, carries the meaning 'pleasing, attractive'; but as L. H. Marshall says, since 'we may perversely find evil things attractive, the rendering "beautiful" is to be preferred'. *Admirable, euphēma*, means not 'well spoken of' but 'speaking well of'; Moffatt's 'high-toned' covers both aspects of the word.

Rather than prolong the list of desirable qualities which should grace the lives of the Philippians the apostle seems to sum up all the virtues which he might have included, in the words: *if anything is excellent or praiseworthy. Excellent (aretē)* in its noun form is a frequent word in classical and Hellenistic Greek, but does not appear elsewhere in Paul, and is found only twice in the remaining New Testament books (1 Pet. 2:9; 2 Pet. 1:3). The word can signify both excellence in any sphere of activity and the prestige which such excellence acquires. *Praiseworthy, epainos*, may be construed as either 'what deserves your praise' or 'anything which calls down the approval of God' (as in Rom. 2:29). In this context, where Paul is employing a list of virtues which represent the best of the contemporary religious world, and especially as seen in the noble types of Roman character, the first meaning is more likely. In L. H. Marshall's words, thus

---

[1] *Cf.* Marshall, *The Challenge of NT Ethics*, pp. 303–305, to be updated by Hawthorne, pp. 187–189.

the term 'praise' is here 'used in its classical sense of universal human approval ... whatever is generally deemed worthy of praise'; and this would appeal to the civic consciousness of his readers, who were living in an outpost of Roman culture and to whom later in the chapter (4:15) he gives their official Roman name, *Philippēsioi* = Latin *Philippenses*.[1]

9. Although the apostle is not unmindful of the darker side of sordidness and vice (see, *e.g.*, Rom. 1:20–32; 1 Cor. 6:9–10; Gal. 5:19–21), he now lists a catalogue of the virtues native to the best 'types' of the world around them. He goes on to set before the Philippians an example of those traits exemplified in a person whom they knew very well: himself. The multiplication of verbs, *learned, received, heard, seen*, shows how well his readers would be able to appreciate his character in which, by the grace of God, the virtues he had enumerated earlier were displayed. As we observed in 3:17, it might appear the height of presumption and egotism on the part of Paul to set down, without apology, his own character and conduct as a standard of behaviour for others. Two things, however, need to be remembered before we jump to this conclusion. There is the qualifying statement of 1 Corinthians 11:1.[2] Then, there is a valuable clue in the term *received, parelabete*, which is a technical term used for the receiving of a tradition (*cf.* 1 Cor. 11:23; 15:3). Before the composition of the New Testament and its acceptance as authoritative Scripture, 'the tradition', as a standard of Christian belief and behaviour, was embodied in the teaching and example of those persons in whose lives the authority and ethical practice of the Lord was to be found. Paul refers to such 'traditions' (or 'commands' or 'ordinances') in a number of places (*cf.* 1 Cor. 11:2; 15:1ff.; Gal. 1:9; Col. 2:6; 1 Thes. 4:1–2; 2 Thes. 2:15). Before they were committed to writing and later formed the corpus of New Testament Scripture they were *learned, received, heard, seen* in the person of the apostles.

A life which is modelled on these patterns of apostolic

[1]For Paul's choice of Roman virtues, see J. N. Sevenster, *Paul and Seneca* (Brill, 1961), pp. 152–156.

[2]On which see W. P. de Boer, *The Imitation of Paul* (Kok, 1962), esp. pp. 169–188.

example and teaching will be blessed with the gift of God's peace (v. 7) which comes from *the God of peace* himself. There is no higher blessing from God; and no finer incentive to 'think about such things' (v. 8).

C. APPRECIATION OF THE PHILIPPIANS' GIFTS (4:10–20)

10. Paul resumes the theme of the letter as a personal message to the church. He now turns his attention to the gift which he had received from Philippi and to the generosity of which the gift is the latest illustration and proof (see note on 1:5). The arrival of the gift at the hands of Epaphroditus (4:18) is made the occasion of rejoicing *in the Lord* who has put this generosity in his people's hearts.

At last suggests a harsh and sinister implication as though Paul were chiding the Philippians for forgetfulness or dilatoriness in sending the money to him. But this idea is absent from the Greek, *ēdē pote* (see Rom. 1:10 for the identical phrase), and the following sentence gives the reason for the unavoidable delay in the arrival of the church's gift.

Michael, followed by Scott, constructs a very elaborate background from the nuances of this paragraph, and sees it as the clearing up of a resentment on the part of the Philippians caused by something Paul had said in a hypothetical first letter of thanks to the church. That these verses do betray a certain tenseness on the apostle's part is undisputed, but this may be explained by his reserve, akin to embarrassment, over money matters in general, which has been detected in 1 Corinthians 9:15–18.[1] The sense of uneasiness results from a conflict between his desire to express sincere appreciation of the help given and a concern to show himself superior to questions of money. In the writer's opinion this natural idiosyncrasy in regard to money, which other servants of God have shared, satisfactorily disposes of the difficulties which Michael raises.

Your concern for me translates *phronein* (lit. 'to think'), a verb

---

[1] See Holmberg, *Paul and Power*, pp. 88–95 on Paul's financial relations with his churches.

used frequently in this letter. See the note on 1:7. It is best rendered in this verse by 'active interest', which the Philippians *have renewed* in their desire and endeavour to send help to the apostle. *Have renewed, anethalete,* which is used only here in the New Testament but found in the LXX, is an interesting word which Paul borrowed from the horticultural practice of his time; it denotes plants and flowers 'blooming again' (*e.g.* Ezk. 17:24). The sense here may be taken in two ways. Either 'you have revived as far as it affects your concern for me' or 'you have revived your concern for me' (so RSV, NIV which is preferred). All the time the Philippians have been *concerned, i.e.* had a thoughtful desire and intention to aid the apostle; but what they lacked was the *opportunity*, the *kairos*, to give expression to their concern (the verb is *ekaireisthe*).

The reason for this absence of favourable circumstances in which they intended to send their help is not stated by Paul. This fact has direct bearing upon the dating of the letter. See the Introduction, pp. 33–34. Whether it was the apostle's situation in some inaccessible place, or the Philippians' own poverty, which prevented the gift reaching him, no blame attached to this failure. It was something outside their control.

11. So the apostle is at pains, at this point, to dispel any thought of personal disappointment or chagrin at the non-arrival of the Philippians' aid, and inserts a parenthesis in verses 11b–13, which is an impressive statement of his 'contentment', *autarkeia*.

He has *learned* the secret of deep peace based on detachment from his outward circumstances. In whatever conditions of life he finds himself, he discovers the will of God for his situation. This is not a fatalism or indolent acquiescence which cuts the nerve of ambition or smothers endeavour, as AV/KJV might suggest. It is, on the contrary, a detachment from anxious concern about the outward features of his life. This, in turn, arises from his concentration upon the really important things, the invisible and eternal (2 Cor. 4:16–18) and, above all, upon the closeness of his fellowship with Christ on whose strength he constantly draws (v. 13).

Content, *autarkēs*, is found only in this verse in the New Testament. As a moral term it plays an important part in the stoic outlook upon life. Socrates, for instance, is held up by Diogenes Laertius in the third century AD as an example of a 'self-sufficient' man who faced, with equanimity and resolution, all that life brought to him. Paul's use of the term is, however, quite distinct from the stoic ideal as verse 13 shows (*cf.* 2 Cor. 9:8). A stoic term may be used; but it is Christ who is the secret of Paul's serenity (1:21). The lesson he learnt came to him in a moment of time, as the aorist tense of the verb indicates. It did not come through patient discipline and concentrated endeavour; it broke upon him at his conversion, and his subsequent career and experience were but the outworking of the intimacy with the living Lord which began at that time. His 'self-sufficiency' derives from the experiential realities of 3:10.

12. Now follows an eloquent description of the apostle's detachment, the repetition of *I know* and the sonorous infinitives, *to be in need*, *to have plenty*, to be *well fed or hungry*, to be *living in plenty or in want*, adding to the impressiveness of the personal testimony. His abasement, *tapeinousthai*, reflects that of his Lord (*cf.* 2:8: 'he humbled himself', *heauton etapeinōsen*) and corroborates his teaching to others (*cf.* 2:3: 'lowliness', *tapeinophrosynē*). It carries the thought of a voluntary acceptance of lowly station, even poverty, for Christ's sake. His disinheritance would follow upon his becoming a Christian, and this is probably in view in 3:7 (*cf.* 1 Cor. 4:10–13; 2 Cor. 6:10). There was also the mental and emotional side of his refusal to assert his right of maintenance from the churches (*cf.* 2 Cor. 11:7).

The opposite of *tapeinousthai* is *to have plenty*, *perisseuein*, lit. 'to overflow', which suggests a life of prosperity. This may refer to his pre-Christian days; or else it may confirm Ramsay's theory that, towards the end of his life, the apostle 'had considerable command of money'.[1] This presupposes a Roman imprisonment as the background of this reference. Ramsay argues that

---

[1]Ramsay, *St. Paul the Traveller and Roman Citizen*, p. 311.

the expenses of his trial at Rome would be heavy and Paul would need to have considerable means at his disposal; but this is largely an assumption. The word may equally signify a possession of spiritual wealth, as in Romans 15:13.

The turn of phrase, *I have learned the secret*, *memyēmai*, uses a technical expression of the pagan mystery cults which employed it of the initiation of their adherents. It is found only here in the New Testament. If the contemporary meaning was in Paul's mind when he wrote the word it might suggest that, as ritual initiation was no easy matter, the school in which he was learning how to face life victoriously was a hard one, a fact which is amply attested in his other writings. His 'initiation' was no ecstastic, secret affair. It meant being willing to be a public spectacle (1 Cor. 4:9ff.) and to undergo all sorts of hardship (2 Cor. 11:23ff.) for Christ's sake.

The kind of life which he experienced as an apostle is described in the verbs which follow. To be *well fed* and to be *hungry* re-echo Jesus' teaching in Luke 6:21, and the best commentary on these poignant words is Paul's *apologia pro vita sua* in 2 Corinthians 11:21ff. The rhythmical pattern of both sets of verses in 2 Corinthians and here is to be noted (Hawthorne, Martin).

13. But there is more to be said about the achievement he has gained. His 'self-sufficiency' and equanimity in meeting all life's demands has not come through a mechanical self-discipline or fixed resolution such as the stoic practised (*cf.* the modern counterpart in Henley's poem 'Invictus'). It was his in union with a personal Lord, whose name is not recorded according to the best MSS (NIV translates therefore: *through him who gives me strength*), but whose influence is unmistakable. The preposition *through*, in fact, is more important than the choice of noun or pronoun.

The spiritual value of this heroic confession is not to be limited to the context, as its place in the life of Oliver Cromwell illustrates. This verse once saved Cromwell's life. It was 'one beam in a dark place' of utter despondency and misery which followed the death of his son. Exegetical considerations, however, require that *everything* must be related to the foregoing verses 11–12. The apostle is insisting that in every conceivable circumstance, 'in any and every situation', he finds the strength which vital union with Christ supplies to be adequate for maintaining his apostolic work and for the fulfilment of his desire to accelerate the progress of the gospel. This statement, then, does not make Paul a wonder-worker, a spiritual 'super-man', who towers so far above the rest of us that his life is no encouragement to lesser mortals. 'Although he was an apostle, he was also a man' is Chrysostom's timely reminder; yet here was a man who had boundless confidence in the ability of Christ to match every situation, and whose 'power' *dynamis* (*cf. endynamounti*, the participle used here), is made perfect in his weakness (2 Cor. 12:9–10). And this means that the triumphant assertion *I can do everything through him who gives me strength* can be true of every Christian today.

14. Paul resumes his treatment of the main theme of the section in recalling appreciatively the church's considerateness in its assistance of his work by their gifts, presumably money. He praises their readiness to *share, synkoinōnēsantes*, with his troubles. *It was good of you*, he writes using an idiomatic turn of phrase. *Kalōs* with aorist tense of the verb expresses a polite request as in Acts 10:33; 3 John 6. The verb defines and illustrates the closeness of this bond which brought and kept together the apostle and his friends. It means 'had fellowship, *koinōnia*, with me', *i.e.* they had identified themselves with the apostle in partnership on behalf of the work of the gospel (see note on 1:5).

My troubles, thlipsis, can hardly mean, in this context, merely 'my difficulties' or 'my personal need'. *Thlipsis* is a technical term for the affliction or tribulation to come on the earth at the end of the age; see Mark 13:19; 2 Thessalonians 1:6. The Philippians, then, by their gifts, may have had a greater honour than just the offer of succour to their apostle; they would be sharing in the apostolic trials which precede and prepare for the end, as Bonnard suggests, as, by their gifts, the gospel is carried to every creature in preparation for that end (Mk. 13:10). This idea, however unusual it may seem at first, holds the key to what follows (v. 15).

15. The historical allusion is to the first preaching of the word in Philippi, recorded in Acts 16, and described here as *the early days of your acquaintance with the gospel* (*cf.* 1:5). It looks back to the day when Paul first ministered the gospel at Philippi. But it also indicates the time of a new 'start' to Paul's apostolic mission.[1]

Moreover, as you Philippians know is a phrase which has been made the basis of Michael's reconstruction of the Philippian correspondence. He sees here a 'note of censure' on the part of the apostle, as though he resented the implication contained in a postulated letter from the Philippians, that he needed to be reminded of his indebtedness to them. The severity of his rebuke is softened by the inserting of the recipients' name as in the case of the Galatians (3:1) and the Corinthians (2 Cor. 6:11). Michael's article may be consulted for further details of this interesting piece of literary detection;[2] but *cf.* the note on 4:10.

The way in which Paul had been assisted by financial gifts is expressed by the verb *shared with* (*cf.* v. 14), *ekoinōnēsen*. The use of this verb shows how the Philippians had demonstrated their partnership with the apostle in his ministry. The bond of Christian affection between them showed itself in the practical expression of their gifts. But are we to understand that Philippi was the only church which aided Paul financially, as Moffatt's translation suggests: 'No church but yourselves had any financial dealings with me'? This rendering, however, obscures the sense of the original where *giving and receiving, doseōs kai lēmpseōs*, refer to a double transaction. Material gifts passed from the church to the apostle, and spiritual blessings flowed the other way. This agrees with 1 Corinthians 9:11 (*cf.* Rom. 15:27). The Philippians were unique in enjoying this two-way transaction: *not one church . . . except you only.*

---

[1] See commentaries of Martin and Hawthorne for what is implied; and the study of Luedemann, *Paul, Apostle to the Gentiles*, pp. 104–107.

[2] Michael, *ExpT*, 24, 1922, pp. 106–109.

The degree of absoluteness about these words will naturally depend upon how we translate the clause, *when I set out from Macedonia*. It could mean that at the time of Paul's departure from Macedonia no other church had fellowship with him by their gifts. Alternatively, the clause may be read, 'when I had left Macedonia', and then the absence of this special feature of *giving and receiving* in Paul's later relations with his churches will mark out the Philippians as in a class apart. For the later help of 'brothers who came from Macedonia' who brought a gift to Paul at Corinth, see 2 Corinthians 11:9; and the help of other churches besides the Philippian church is implied in 2 Corinthians 11:8; 12:13. He refused to accept gifts from the Corinthian church (1 Cor. 9:15-27; 2 Cor. 11:9).[1]

16. For the apostle's ministry at Thessalonica see Acts 17:1-9. The question raised by this verse hinges on the time of the Philippians' gifts and the precise connotation of *again and again*. As Paul had cause to refer to his 'toil and hardship' (1 Thes. 2:9; 2 Thes. 3:8) at Thessalonica, it is likely that the gifts which came to him there made little difference to his economic condition. *Even* recalls with gratitude the speed with which the help came so soon after his departure from Philippi. The phrase *again and again, kai hapax kai dis*, can only mean 'more than once' (Moffatt) with no indication of the exact number of times.[2] If the first word *kai* ('and') is not part of the expression (it is not translated in NIV), but rather a connective word, then the sense will be: 'Both when I was at Thessalonica and more than once when I was in other places' you sent a gift to help me in my need, *chreia*.

17. The presence of commercial terms is noticeable in this verse as Paul calls to mind the generosity of the church. He, however, disclaims any covetous seeking for gifts (2 Cor. 12:14); and this clear statement of his disinterested attitude in regard to

---

[1]Holmberg, *Paul and Power*, p. 94, has argued that it was the Corinthian church, not the Philippians, who proved to be the exception; so the first view stated above is the more likely.

[2]See L. Morris' article on the phrase in *NovT*, 1, 1956, pp. 205-208; and *I and II Thessalonians* (*Tyndale New Testament Commentaries*, IVP/Eerdmans, 1984), p. 23.

money will have been necessary if, at this time, he was being accused of underhand methods (see Introduction, p. 33). His concern was rather for *what may be credited to your account*. The key words are all current commercial expressions. *Karpos* is a Greek word not separately translated in NIV; its meaning is 'fruit' in the sense of 'interest' accruing to a financial account; *credited, pleonazonta; account, logos* (which in 4:15 is translated as 'in respect to' giving and receiving). Moule brings out the commercial flavour with his translation: 'the interest which is accruing to your credit'. What the Philippians gave as their *gift* was like an investment which would repay rich dividends in the service of the kingdom, as accumulating interest (*karpos; cf.* Moulton-Milligan on a related word with *karpeia*) stands to the credit (*logos*) of the depositor. At the last day such generous and unstinted service which expressed itself in practical monetary support would not go unrecognized or unrewarded (*cf.* 1:11). This is the ambition of Paul for his benefactors: it is surely a most remarkable way of saying 'Thank you' to the Philippians.

18. Financial terminology is continued in the apostle's admission, *I have received full payment and even more*. The evidence of the papyri throws much light on the special meaning of *I have received, apechō*.[1] The current sense was 'here, then, is my receipt' (GNB), used as a technical expression for the drawing up of a receipt in business (*cf.* Mt. 6:5; Mk. 14:41). *And even more* translates the verb, *perisseuō* (*cf.* 4:12) which completes the sense with Paul's acknowledgment that their generosity has more than covered his need (4:16).

I am amply supplied, peplērōmai, continues the admission that all his material requirements have been met in the service the Philippians have rendered to him, and refutes the charge of any ingratitude or thoughtlessness on his part. This is especially clear in the way in which he describes the gift which came by *Epaphroditus* (*cf.* 2:25), who was the bearer of it, as being *acceptable* in the eyes of God. If God were pleased with it as an

[1] See Deissmann, *Light from the Ancient East*, pp. 111, 112, 331; Barclay, *New Testament Words*, pp. 17–20.

acceptable sacrifice, pleasing to him, surely the Philippians must believe that the apostle too was truly thankful and appreciative. The language used to describe their gift, as *a fragrant offering*, is taken from the Old Testament (Gn. 8:21; *cf.* Ex. 29:18; Lv. 1:9, 13; Ezk. 20:41), and is a reminder to us that all sincere Christian service which entails sacrificial and self-denying cost not only promotes the cause of Christ and strengthens the hand of God's servants, but it is an act of worship in which God takes pleasure.

Although financial and transactional terms have been used of the church's gift, the apostle now lifts the minds of his readers above the actual sending and receiving of the gift to the spirit which has prompted it and the purpose which it ultimately served. No doubt he uses the commercial terms in a playful or, at best, illustrative sense. The idea, however, of the church's ready help and his own indebtedness is put on the highest level possible by the solemn words which characterize it as a *sacrifice pleasing to God*. The reward of all our service and our stewardship is to have pleased him (2 Cor. 5:9).

19. The connection with the preceding verse is given as *and* (or 'but', 'in return'), *de*, which suggests that the Philippians had helped the apostle to their own impoverishment. This may well have been the case if 2 Corinthians 8:2ff. is the appropriate background of the letter. Now, Paul reassures them, God will not fail to meet their need as they have not been remiss in meeting his. Michaelis takes this view, citing 2 Corinthians 8:2 as evidence of the 'present external, distressed condition' of the Philippian church at that time. Support for his view is found in the use of the words *will meet*, *plērōsei* (which is the same term as the verb translated 'I am amply supplied' in v. 18) and *needs*, *chreia*, which is again used of the apostle's need in 4:16 and earlier in 2:25. On this reading, what Paul is holding out to his Philippian friends is a reassurance of the faithfulness of God who, as he has supplied the material need of his servant, is able to supply all their needs too. The precise meaning of *will meet* as a wish-prayer, not a statement of fact, is a helpful insight.[1]

---

[1]Hawthorne, p. 208 citing Wiles, *Paul's Intercessory Prayers*, pp. 101–107.

But it would be wrong to exclude the thought of the provision of God for their spiritual needs, and possibly both types of need are in mind in the addition of *all*. Whatever their deficiency may be, God will supply the remedy. 'You have generously supplied my physical requirements by your gifts,' the apostle is saying. 'God is the rewarder of such self-sacrificing service. He who is *my God* will not disappoint you in the full supply of whatever need you have.' In fact, the source and extent of this divine supply are given in some profound words: *according to his glorious riches in Christ Jesus*. We may notice, following Michael, that the measure of God's provision as expressed in the preposition *according to*, *kata*, makes it clear that 'the rewarding will not be merely from His wealth, but also in a manner that befits His wealth – on a scale worthy of His wealth'. Who can estimate the range and depth of this richness (see Rom. 11:33)? Every conceivable human need is more than adequately supplied from such a source.

The exact force of *glorious* (lit. 'in glory') is open to different interpretations. It may be construed adverbially as qualifying *meet* with the meaning: 'supply in a glorious manner'; or it may point forward to the glory reserved for believers in the future kingdom of God: 'in the glory' (see Motyer). More probably, however, it is to be connected with *riches*. The phrase will then mean *glorious riches*. The two words, *riches*, *glory*, are more or less synonyms according to certain meanings of *glory* (*kabōd* in Hebrew) in the Old Testament. Compare Genesis 31:1 and Isaiah 10:3, where 'glory' is equivalent to wealth, riches, as in NIV.

The richness of God's mercy and provision is made known *in Christ Jesus*. In him, God's full wealth of revelation and redemption (Col. 1:27; 2:3) is contained, so that we are 'rich' in him (2 Cor. 8:9), *i.e.* in union with him by faith, and thereby linked to the source and supply of all true wealth.

20. The outburst of doxology prolongs the theme of God's *glory* which is ascribed to him who is *our God and Father*. The thought now is one of praise rendered to God in acknowledgement of thankfulness for all his goodness and grace. It expresses, too, Paul's own gratitude for the response of God's people to his need, and the intimate fellowship with them in his gospel ministry. 'The doxology flows from the joy of the whole Epistle', says Bengel, *i.e.* it is Paul's fitting response to all the things which cause him joy in his prison experience. The liturgical *Amen*, lit. 'confirmed', derived from a Hebrew verb 'to be firm', underlies the truth of the doxology, as the writer and reader associate themselves with the confession and own it as valid and true for themselves.

D. GREETINGS (4:21–22)

21–22. Final greetings are sent to the church which is honoured by the title *all the saints* (*cf.* the phrase in 1:1). Paul is careful, as throughout the entire letter, to include the whole Christian community at Philippi within the scope of his pastoral care. The verb *greet, aspasasthe*, is repeated as *send you greetings* in the second sentence. *The brothers*, fellow-Christians in the place of his confinement and including Timothy, join him in a Christian salutation. This was a practice borrowed from the letter-writing habits of the ancient world, but filled with a Christian content.[1]

Among the Christian believers who are identified with Paul in his greeting, although we should not suppose that they were actually in prison with him, a special group is singled out for particular mention, *those who belong to Caesar's household*. The occasion of this greeting may conceivably have been the link of special interest between the Christian members of the imperial staff on government service at the place of Paul's imprisonment and the Christian citizens of Philippi which was a Roman military colony. The reference to *Caesar's household* (the Greek words, *hoi ek tēs Kaisaros oikias* would be equivalent to the Latin *familia Caesaris*) has been regarded as confirming the Roman

---

[1] See Doty, *Letters in Primitive Christianity*; E. E. Ellis, 'Paul and his co-workers' in his *Prophecy and Hermeneutic in Early Christianity* (Eerdmans, 1978), pp. 13–22; but for another view see Ollrog, *Paulus and seine Mitarbeiter*, p. 78.

captivity of the apostle as the background of the letter; but it is clear that it cannot mean the family of the emperor or members of the court circles at Rome. The translation 'Imperial slaves' (Moffatt) unduly narrows this group to the slaves by omitting other members of the freedmen class, unless 'slaves' is taken in the broader sense of 'servants', *i.e.* civil servants. See some evidence drawn from Romans 16:3–16 in Bruce. But the term is flexible, and could include those in government service in any city including Ephesus (Getty).

The state of affairs which has just been described would equally apply to Ephesus where there is inscriptional evidence of the presence of 'Caesar's house', *i.e.* members of 'Government House', in the service of the emperor as civil servants and government officials. Dibelius quotes an inscription showing how members of the civil service, both freedmen and slaves, formed themselves into *collegia* or guilds as servants of 'our Lord Augustus'.

No decisive result on the question of the locality of Paul's place of writing can be gained, therefore, from this verse.

E. BENEDICTION (4:23)

23. The concluding benediction is in the typical Pauline manner. *The grace of the Lord Jesus Christ* crowns the entire letter, and forms the apostle's prayer for his 'joy and crown', his 'beloved' fellowship of the saints of God at Philippi (4:1). He desires that the grace of the one who is the theme of his own life (1:21) and the subject-matter of his epistle may be *with your spirit* (added following the best MSS).

The final *Amen* (*cf.* 4:20) is dropped by most modern editors of the text, but it has strong attestation.[1] In any case, it forms a fitting response to the apostle's prayer for the church at Philippi – and for the church of Jesus Christ in every place and age.

[1] Details are given in Hawthorne, p. 212.